D0173218

RECIPES FROM PARENTING

Sandy Spurgeon McDaniel

SPURGEON HOUSE PUBLICATION
a division of
SANDY MCDANIEL ENTERPRISES
P.O. Box 15458
Newport Beach, CA 92660
(714) 642-3605

Cover photography by
Western Images, Newport Beach, CA

Typing and book layout by
Pat Davidson and Kaveh Esteghamat
Typeline, Costa Mesa, CA

TECHNICAL ADVISORS:
Ginny Barnett, Judy Bauer, Claire & Dwight Belden,
Bruce Bracken, Barbara K. Carr, Judy Coyne, Nancy Coyne,
Barbara Jean, Jaclyn Johnson, Jan Kingaard, Dr. Darlene Landis,
Mary Pat Lucas, Ann Obegi, Susan Smith,
Kathleen Spurgeon and Shelley Spurgeon.

Cover: Kathleen & Scott's original handprints

Second Printing
©1990 Sandy S. McDaniel

All rights reserved.
No part of this book may be
reproduced or transmitted in any
form including photocopying, recording
or by information storage and retrieval
system without permission in writing
by the publisher.

ISBN 0-9626359-1-X

Printed in the USA by
Publishers Press
Salt Lake City, Utah

*For all we have taught and learned from
each other, for all the mistakes each of us has made,
for their courage in being unwilling to compromise
on their own truth, and for the incomprehensible joy
of loving and having been loved by them....
I heartfully dedicate this book to my two children,
<u>Kathleen and Scott McDaniel</u>*

RECIPES FROM PARENTING . . . is the first book to be published by SPURGEON HOUSE. The name SPURGEON HOUSE is chosen to honor and thank my parents, Kay and Bill Spurgeon for all they taught me and for always loving me.

The banner never hit the ground, Dad!

INTRODUCTION

The most heart-warming, challenging, fearful, frustrating, rewarding times you will ever know happen within the realm of responsibility called PARENTING.

No parent I know ever gets up in the morning with the thought, "Wonder what I can do to mess up my kid's life today," and yet we all know how easy it is to emotionally harm these fragile beings called children. So we head into our parenting years burdened with the "shoulds" from our parents (who lived in an altogether different age), our own personal fears and an overwhelming lack of guidance in terms of education. No wonder many of us lie awake nights, fraught with worry!

As the parent of a seventeen year old son (Scott) and a nineteen year old daughter (Kathleen) it is obvious to me that the work I have done to enhance their self-esteem has been the key factor in their success as human beings.

Self-concept is a picture you have about yourself, given to you primarily through messages from other people in the form of "you" messages: You are thoughtful, lazy, worthless, dependable, etc. Self-esteem is the way you **feel** about the picture you have of yourself.

Self-esteem is the basis for every choice you make: Whether you take risks, the friends you choose, how you handle success and failure, whether you do well in school and in life. Self-esteem is a feeling, and since feelings can change, one can effectively influence and enhance a person's self-esteem.

Twelve years of research went into co-authoring an elementary school program called PROJECT SELF-ESTEEM (available through a non-profit organization, Enhancing Education, Inc. PO Box 16001, Newport Beach, CA. 92659). This successful program has proven again and again that **lack of awareness is the same as no choice.** Given specific skills for their every-day lives, youth respond and take responsibility for their choices. Children who feel good about themselves learn better, exhibit more constructive behavior, are more supportive towards each other and tend to refrain from such self-destructive choices as drug use.

From my perspective, the number one contribution to a child's sense of self-esteem comes from his/her parents. Giving your child a sense of feeling LOVABLE (loved no matter what his/her choices may be) and CAPABLE (able to do some things well) is the strongest foundation you can build for the many challenges and pressures in children's lives.

This book is about strengthening your child's sense of feeling lovable and capable. *It is not a book on theory, but on practical application of parenting techniques and especially communication skills that have worked for me.*

When my daughter Kathleen was eleven and my son Scott was nine, we got a divorce. Though this book is written mostly from my reference as a single parent, the skills are of equal value to both mothers and fathers.

I play with small children and babies in the market, and my message to their mothers is one you will hear throughout this book: ON YOUR WORST DAY, REMEMBER THAT THIS TIME WITH YOUR CHILDREN GOES TOO FAST.

In the time of "used-to-be" Kathleen would bring a book and snuggle into my lap, content just to read and be with me. Today, at nineteen, she has her own car, a job, goes to college and spends whatever time she can with her boyfriend. I would carry Scott around on my hip; today he is almost six foot five. He and my car are gone a lot. There were a lot of days, many struggles, lots of misunderstanding, tons of fun and love in the days since those of my early memories — and I still marvel that I have a daughter who is nineteen and a son who is seventeen. How can it be? Trust me, it goes too fast.

In the days of "used-to-be" I would have sold my house for just a few minutes to myself. Today, both cars are gone from the garage, I often eat dinners alone, and I often go to bed at night before my teenagers return from their activities. In the hallway are pictures with strings of memories attached. I have lots of free minutes now. My considerable investment of time in the days of "used to be" are continually paying off.

The world isn't doing very well. Drug use is escalating. Moral decay is rampant. Compassion and kindness are endangered species in a world that cannot survive without them. We feel helpless at the scope of such problems. I believe that God wants us to save our world, and that we must begin by molding strong youth who will then make choices for a new way of living. As parents of small children, you hold the quality of life for all of us in your hands. Every minute of caring and coaching you contribute to your child is also a contribution towards a better way of life for all of us.

This book is about the struggles and the joys of being a parent. It is practical, usable information for you in your own role as a parent. It is a gift from my awareness and my heart to yours.

Sandy S. McDaniel

TABLE OF CONTENTS

RECIPES FROM PARENTING

- A recipe is one person's version of how to combine ingredients towards an end product.
- Recipes may be changed to fit the taste of each individual.
- Often recipes are perfected by experimentation and change.
- Essential ingredients in recipes for parenting are:

> LISTEN TO YOUR OWN INSTINCTS
>
> BE WILLING TO BE IMPERFECT AND MAKE MISTAKES
>
> REMEMBER: LOVE WORKS, EVERYTHING ELSE DOESN'T

The world changed very rapidly. Massive confusion is the result of that change, especially in the area of raising children. Our parents had specific parts in their play called life; their role and even their lines were determined by a script that all of them followed. Suddenly, we found ourselves in a world which is totally different from that of our own youth. The way we were parented doesn't completely fit with parenting the children of today. For us as parents, it is like walking onto a stage, having someone take the script away, being aware our line is coming up and we don't even know what the play is about! To add to this drama, as parents we desperately want to teach our children to be safe in a world in which we do not feel safe. No wonder we're terrified by the awesome responsibility those tiny beings bring to our life!

I have no idea how to cure the ills of the world. I do have some thoughts about how to parent your children so they feel loved.

Please regard these thoughts as "thought provokers" to your own parenting. If something you read assists you in better understanding your role or your children, I am glad. I am not a psychologist, I am a mother who likes to write. In the twelve years of traveling nationally and internationally giving workshops on parenting and self-esteem, I've talked to thousands of parents about their common concerns. In addressing those concerns from my own frame of reference I use my gift of writing for the purpose it was given: to assist others.

The following pages may not be your truths — they are mine.

BASIC INFORMATION

COMFORT ZONES

Essential Ingredients:
Understanding • Perspective • Attitude

Remember: Asking yourself what might be happening underneath a behavior can change your perspective thus the way you respond to your child.

Hold your left hand up so it is parallel to the floor (as if you were going to salute from your chest). Hold your right hand below the left one so they are parallel to each other.

Your left hand represents how much positive or good you can handle in your life. The right hand represents how much negative or bad you can handle in your life. The space between your two hands is known as your comfort zone.

As you are aware, you can have a very large comfort zone about some things (cooking dinner or maybe fixing the car) and an very small comfort zone about something else (speaking in front of people for instance). How large a comfort zone you have is usually based upon a past experience.

A friend of mine who is an eloquent speaker and had just given the keynote address at a major conference, was a bundle of nerves when I picked her up to go where we were to be on a live television program. Why? The last time she was on television, she had said something that was incorrect and had been called on it. Her comfort zone for being on live TV went from very large to very small in one experience.

When a child balks or is otherwise afraid, he or she is experiencing a small comfort zone. That awareness gives you a new perspective. Your job is to provide a positive experience so his/her comfort zone increases in that specific area.

Remember, emotional damage may occur if you say, "Hey, there's nothing to be afraid of! That's easy!" or "Why are you afraid?" ("I just am!" is probably the only response you will hear.) All of those are crippling words of judgment. Instead, wrap the child in kindness and assist him/her in heading for a new experience.

Maybe simple words like, "Tell me about your fear," or "What is the scariest thing about (what is happening)?" can build a bridge so your child takes a vital step in overcoming fears: admitting they exist.

PRACTICE: LEARNING TO RESPECT COMFORT ZONES

TO DO: Write each person's name (in the family) vertically on a piece of paper. Divide the rest of the paper into two columns. In the first column, write, "HIGH" and in the other column write, "LOW".

Discuss as parents or (depending on the ages of your children), areas where each individual has a high or low comfort zone. This exercise must be void of any judgment whatsoever. The value is to increase understanding thus tolerance among individual family members.

Name	High	Low
Mom	cooking tennis writing	parties
Dad	at work sports	talking
Kathleen	school writing	being teased
Scott	sports talking	speaking to groups

REMEMBER: DO NOT ALLOW ANY JUDGMENTAL STATEMENTS FROM ANY FAMILY MEMBER

No: "You're too old to be afraid of the dark!"
Yes: "Lots of people are afraid of the dark."

No: "You're not afraid of speaking. You've talked to lots of groups."
Yes: "Does this one (speaking to groups) mean that you are scared of speaking and you do it anyway? Cool."

RESPECT THE SMALL CHILD WITHIN

> Essential Ingredients:
> Awareness • Patience • Compassion

Remember: The small child needs to be honored.

Every single one of us has inside of us a small child. That child usually ranges between two and four years old. It never gets any older. Left unattended or put on a shelf, this child can be a troublemaker.

Your child inside becomes visible when you are pouting, want to get even, have irrational thoughts or want to ride on a carrousel but wouldn't be caught dead doing so without a child. It is the part of you that plays games with people rather than just being you, has expectations that are not reasonable, is a task master with yourself, and the part of you that has been wounded. At the same time, your small child is the delightful, spontaneous, truthful, free spirit that you probably were as an infant.

As a parent, our job is to teach our child's small child inside to feel safe so it doesn't contaminate the bright spirit with which it was born. Hopefully this book is filled with ideas for nurturing your child's small child inside.

Knowing that your child has a small child inside can give you a different perspective, especially when you want to strangle your little dear. "Your small child is on a terror today" is a different thought than, "Why is he/she trying to drive me crazy?"

Say to a stormy child, "You're really angry about not being able to have that candy bar. Being angry is OK, throwing a fit is not. Why don't you help me put the groceries on the counter so we can go home?" Such words honor the infant's feelings without letting the small child control the situation. Note the verbal suggestion for something else to do: Stubbornness is enhanced by leaving a child with only the alternative to mind or not to mind. Rerouting the child's attention sometimes works and—sometimes doesn't.

When you come up against being embarrassed in the store by your child's behavior remember: what other people think of you as a parent is none of your business. Your child's training and the relationship you are building with your child are more valuable than the vote of the whole community. Besides, your child will know if you give in under the pressure of public opinion, and then you are in for it!

AGES AND STAGES

> Essential Ingredient:
> Awareness • Patience • Kindness

Remember: No two children are alike — an overview of ages and stages is given as a guideline NOT as a measurement.

Only 50% of children at age 3 are able to share. Most of us decide to socialize our little ones at age 2, wondering why so little visiting time occurs for the adults and the play is substantially lacking in harmony. It is wise to have a visiting child bring his or her own toy, ideally for sharing and also for play if "what's mine is mine" becomes the name of the game for that day.

Here, from my research, are some concepts that may assist:

1. Age 2: Must practice separateness. Accept defiant feelings but re-channel defiant behavior.

2. Ages 3-5: Attachment to parent of opposite sex. Be sure to have and honor a "stop" signal for any stimulating behavior like tickling.

3. Age 3-6: Shows growing pride over accomplishments. Provide experiences that lend themselves to success. Give lots of encouragement and compliments, with as little correcting as possible. Attachment to parent of opposite sex.

4. Age 6: Very self-centered. Prefer own-sexed parent. Conscience begins to take shape.

5. Ages 6-12: Interest moves outside of family. Time of pals and crushes. Sameness is essential. Withhold information from parents — secrets. Tall tales if there's a need for attention. Find adult model (hero) outside of home.

> THE FIRST BORN: More conservative, more organized, loner, achiever, perfectionist.
> THE SECOND BORN: Competitive more flexible, social, rebellious, less consistent, helpless.
> YOUNGEST: Out-going, social, manipulative, demanding sometimes helpless.
> ONLY CHILD: Adult-oriented, difficulty with peers, conscientious.
> MIDDLE CHILD: Twice replaced; vacillates between being older and the baby, difficulty establishing own identity.

The value of noting ages and stages is to release you from the fear that your child's behavior is necessarily reflective of some misguided parenting skill. No two children are alike!

UNDERNEATH FEELING

```
Essential Ingredients:
Awareness • Understanding • Compassion
```

Remember: Feelings that are demonstrated in negative behavior are a cry for assistance.

At the risk of boxing in and labeling something that needs to be constantly measured off of **what you know to be true for YOUR child**, I offer the following ideas for assistance:

1. Anger is a natural feeling which is not wrong — the behavior you choose to use may be constructive or destructive. Angry feelings that are held inside tend to take over and control other feelings.

2. Depression is often anger or sadness that is repressed. Guilt which is unexpressed can turn to sadness and then to depression.

3. Defensiveness comes from a lack of self-assurance. A child who is always defensive probably feels like he/she can't do much that is right.

4. Embarrassment can be delight and fear next to each other. Though this feeling looks "charming", it can set up a negative experience on which life decisions are made.

5. Envy is wanting what someone else has or wanting to be like someone else. Sometimes envy can be re-channeled by focusing on personal strengths rather than trying to adapt to be like someone else.

6. Fear is worry about loss or harm. Some fears come from a past experience. Admitting you are afraid is the beginning of conquering fear rather than it conquering you.

7. Guilt most often occurs when anger is not expressed. Sometimes, guilt has to do with not doing something that "should have been done". Feeling you let someone down brings guilt. Children who are filled with guilt often become self-destructive.

8. Hurt usually comes from loss, the fear of loss or the decision that loss has occurred.

9. Jealousy is wanting someone to feel towards you what is felt towards someone else. Envy or fear cause jealousy.

10. Loneliness usually comes from feeling unlovable.

CHILDREN ARE FOREVER CHANGING

> Essential Ingredients:
> Flexibility • Patience • Awareness

Remember: Change is a process, it takes time and is always stressful.

From my journal:

The house is empty, much too clean

On the counters and floors no toys can be seen

Bicycle's gone, both beds are made

The jug in the frig is filled with lemonade

The dog's alone in the backyard

To hear any noise you must listen very hard

Though it makes me look like a fool

It's tough getting used to them going back to school!

Change. An endless part of your parenting is dealing with change. You change from doing whatever you want to keeping a schedule that includes a baby. You change to a kid-watcher when the child begins to move. You change to the answer-person when your child starts to talk. You change from being the only playmate to trying to teach your child to play with others. You may change from having one child to having more children. You change from having the children around all day to brief periods of time in which he/she/they go to school. You change to longer periods of time when the children are in school. You change to being the person your children share with to the person who is ignored. You change from having your children spend the night elsewhere to having endless children spending the night at your house. You change from children who eat very little to children (especially boys) who eat everything. You change from having everyone home every night to having no one home for dinner. You change from having all your children at home to having one go off to college. You change your whole life when the last one goes off to college. You change when..........

The above is a mere outline of possible changes that can occur. Being flexible is not only helpful but a necessity. You will stretch your boundaries beyond comprehension, spend days wondering if it will ever end, abstain from murder or child abuse, wonder if there is ever such a thing as one moment of time just for you — and then there are lots of moments just for you. Adapt to change the best you can and...

REMEMBER, EACH STAGE IS TEMPORARY; LIVE ONE DAY AT A TIME. *YOU* ARE CHANGING TOO, SO ALLOW YOURSELF TO MAKE MISTAKES. *CHANGE IS A PROCESS.*

NOT PASSING ON YOUR FAMILY MISTAKES

> Essential Ingredients:
> Listening • Awareness • Allow Mistakes

Remember: The sins of the father (the mistakes made by the parents) are cast upon the son (are passed down from generation to generation).

• Having been raised in an authoritarian home it was very traumatic for me to change that pattern and raise my children in a way which honors my own beliefs. Even though there was no way I could do my parenting exactly the same way, I lived with a fear in the back of my mind that some day one of my children would make a major mistake and a large hand would come out of the sky with the words, "SEE! YOU DID IT WRONG!"

With a seventeen year old son and nineteen year old daughter I'm not out of the woods yet...and I no longer wait for the hand.

• One of the most noticeable areas of inherited traits is found in the realm of eating. Parents who are overweight have an 80% higher chance of having overweight children. Why? We teach the most by modeling. Eating everything on your plate, being rewarded for behavior with food, being punished with food, the type of food eaten, and many more aspects of eating are passed down from generation to generation. Look at your own eating patterns and ask yourself where you got them. Parents, right? It is not easy to discover your patterns and equally difficult not to pass them down to your children.

• The other day I was feeling very agitated. Scott came in and I assaulted him with, "My car is a mess. Clean it or you're not going to be driving it again!"

Having walked past me, he backed up asking with raised eyebrows, "Excuse me?"

I saw that "inherited tactics" were being used and quickly responded, "Sorry, pal, that's my past talking. I noticed that there is a lot of trash and clothes in my car and I want you to clean it up today."

"I already did, at noon," was all the truth Scott needed to say to end our now-adult conversation.

• It is really difficult not to fall back into learned patterns of responding. When you do, catch yourself, identify the error and ask for an instant rerun. (See page 79).

PRACTICE: GETTING IN TOUCH WITH THINGS PASSED DOWN TO YOU FROM GENERATION TO GENERATION

The easiest way to get in touch with what has been passed down to you is to take a piece of paper and divide it into at least four categories: home, job, relationships, and parent. Then write in each square, "I **should**" and think of a should pertaining to that category. Make a list in each square of your "shoulds". Then switch to another PRISON word: **ought, must, have to** and **everybody**, and add to your list of shoulds. When you are finished, go back and put a check by any sentence in which you hear your mother or father (or significant adult) talking. Not all the injunctions you find will be wrong or even negative; the point is to see what you are carrying from your past and choose if you want to pass those ideas onto your children.

HOME	JOB
I should keep the house clean, always	I should do things on time
I must do things right	I must not make mistakes
I have to do everything so my children will love me.	Everybody should work as hard as I do.
RELATIONSHIPS	AS A PARENT WITH CHILDREN
I should understand	I should be more strict
I must be kind, always	I must feed my children dinner by six o'clock
I should never show or talk about my anger because I will not be loved if I do.	I have to be strict even if it means being unreasonable.

EXAMPLES OF CHANGING TO A NEW WAY OF DOING THINGS

> Essential Ingredients:
> Awareness • Patience • Self-trust

Remember: Changing patterns is not disrespect. If each generation improves on the past choices, society gets better, not stagnant.

My father thought that Mother's Day and Father's Day were silly traditions trumped up by the card people to sell merchandise. In a family where there is continual honoring and celebration, there is no need for such a special day. And yet, to children, such days are important.

Carrying on my family beliefs, I have tried to talk down Mothers Day. Last year, I even gave my children the injunction that they were to do nothing about the upcoming celebration for mothers. The night before Mother's Day, there was a gift on my opened bed with a card that read, "I am picking this unofficial day to tell you that I love you and that I think you are the best mommy in the whole world! I love you! Kathleen."

• Somewhere in my late thirties, I realized I got out of bed every morning and made my bed because my mother made me do that as a child. After a significant period of time where I crawled out of bed and shamefully left it unmade, I went back to making the bed as I crawl out each morning. I like the look of the room with the bed made (and it is easier to stack stuff on the bed if it is made!). My children were asked to make their beds as small children. I still ask that beds be made, and deliberately overlook it when they are not. In Scott's room, one does not notice the unmade bed as the whole room is a disaster. He long ago gave up top sheets for a comforter and sleeps in underwear plus a T-shirt. Now he cleverly slings the comforter over the bed (which is flat on the floor without box springs), and the remaining blanket covers some of the mess (or so he thinks).

• The most difficult areas for me to change are in expecting total obedience without comment, never expressing anger, eating whether you are hungry or not, and not having a right to your own feelings. Day-by-day, listening to what I say, watching my children respond, and most importantly giving my children the right to say what they are thinking, I learn from my mistakes. Rather than making my parents wrong, I am parenting in a way that works for me. I am grateful to my parents for all they taught me; this is simply improving on something that had both strengths and weaknesses. In that way perhaps, my children have an even better chance than I did to be more than survivors in a world of many changes.

LITTLE SQUIRTS

NEW BABY COMING: JEALOUSY

Essential Ingredients:
Compassion • Patience • Communication

**Remember: If a child displays signs of jealousy, the
child is sending a message, usually of fear.**

Fact: The single child has a great "gig" going; two adults think
he/she is the greatest thing since sliced bread and pay attention only to
the one child. Why then, as a small child, would it be good news to hear
that there will soon be another little creature (maybe even cuter than I
am) to divide the attention ratio?

I remember being concerned that Kathleen would be jealous of
the new baby. Her father and I called it "our baby" and we included her
in most of our plans. (In those days, we didn't know what sex the baby
would be.)

M: "Kathleen, we are thinking about putting the new baby into the
    bassinet and then we could have the baby in any room we want."
K: "Can the new baby sleep in my room?"
M: "New babies cry in the night because they are hungry. It might be
    better to put our baby in the empty room and then we could put
    him or her in your bed first thing in the morning."
K: "I could read stories to our baby."
M: "Oh, that would be so helpful. Do you think you might help give
    our baby a bath and feed our baby, too?"
K: "Can I get in the tub with our baby?"
M: "Well, a baby is small like your doll, so we will use a plastic bath
    for our baby. You could help me wash our baby."
K: "I want to buy a present for our baby. What can I get?"
M: "Why don't we make a list of things we will need and then you
    can pick one thing for you to give our baby."

For us, the intent was to include Kathleen in the care taking of the
new baby. We bought a photo album, she decided the color. We looked at
pictures in a book and talked about how the baby was developing. We
spent lots of time getting ready for "our" baby.

On the day baby Scott was brought home, the front door opened
and Kathleen ran inside. She got just to the hallway door, headed for
where I was sitting on the couch, and a yowl from down the hall caught
her ear. Turning on one foot, she was gone from sight. When we got to
her (she was two years old) she was half-way into the bassinet, ardently
holding Scott's hand and talking a blue streak about all the things we
were going to do together. They have been best friends from day one —
after all, it was her baby, too.

PARENTAL TEAMWORK

Essential Ingredients: Communication • Allowing • Time and Patience

Remember: It is absolutely essential that parents agree on each and every policy for raising their children.

The relationship between mother and father is tested many times throughout the childhood years. It is essential that parents work out their differences of opinion away from the children's view. Inconsistent policies teach children to play one parent off of the other. Consistency builds a foundation of strength and moral fiber which assists children in making wise choices for their lives.

Reading a parenting book together (even a chapter at a time) and discussing it, sets into motion the idea of working together. If this action occurs prior to the birth of a child, such bonding will assist your husband in whatever feelings he may have about being displaced by a baby.

Mothers who stay home with children often have difficulty communicating with their husband. How much conversation can you make about the baby woke, ate, pooped, got a bath and went back to sleep? Too often, the male has no room for such drivel in the scope of his world-solving problems. So a communication breakdown begins. One reason it is important that a couple continue to do outside things is to give them common ground for communication.

There is no way a man understands what your day (which looks easy compared to his) can have in the way of stress. Besides, you will note that your baby will sleep erratically on Monday-Friday but takes lo-ong naps on Saturday and Sunday, when Dad is babysitting. I can remember returning from shopping thinking of my husband struggling to get Kathleen to sleep, later coping with diapers, snacks, etc. only to come home and find him half-asleep, watching golf on TV. "She's still asleep?" I'd asked, "She must've taken forever to go down....What? She went right down you say..." Bang!

Every skill required by an executive, psychologist, marketing person, sanitary engineer, coach, teacher, nurse, nutritionist, decorator, shopper and about ten other jobs is incorporated into the one job of being a mother. I remember some salesperson asking, "Then just your husband works?" Gently, I replied, " We are equally employed; I'm the one with the courage — I stay home with the kids!"

Wives, whether your husband gets this or not...you do!

GETTING A BABY-SITTER

> Essential Ingredients:
> Thinking Ahead • Listening • Instinct

Remember: Your small child identifies safety with your presence — for some children being left is a major drama.

Kathleen thought baby-sitters were wonderful! Having someone to play games with, read with, snuggle with and talk to was never a source of concern for her. Scott however, screamed for the first two hours, every time we left him. Though he would settle down eventually, he was clearly not thrilled with the idea of having his mother leave him.

Eventually, Scott got over his need to cry when a baby-sitter came. The bottom line is that parents have a right to a life other than that with children. Getting a baby-sitter the children like, one who is responsible and one who relates to children are important considerations in this sometimes arduous process of taking time for yourself.

Your children are irreplaceable. Think of the guilt you would have if an incompetent baby-sitter was the cause of extreme harm. I think it is essential to interview a baby-sitter:

1. For which other families do you baby-sit?
2. Have you stayed with children age (your children's ages) before?
3. What do you think you would do if one of my children fell and was bleeding badly? (This question shows you if the teenager has the resource of responding to danger.)
4. What do you charge per hour?

Essential information to give the baby-sitter up-front and to leave with him/her when you leave are:

1. Exactly what you expect to be done. (Feeding the children, doing dishes, etc. need to be mentioned.)
2. Expectations: Bed time, snacks and limitations in terms of where they can go outside, need to be noted.
3. The name and phone # where you may be reached and the name and phone # of one neighbor who could assist if there were an emergency.
4. The phone # of the fire department, police department and local hospital need to be immediately available.

Remember, you are asking a teenager to have the ability to deal with the little dramas that can drive you up the wall. The more support you give, the more safety you provide for your children when you leave.

ASSISTING CHILDREN WHO DO NOT LIKE TO BE LEFT

> Essential Ingredients:
> Communication • Keep Your Word • You Let Go!

Remember: Rejection and abandonment are basal fears of most human beings; it is difficult for some children to get over the fear of separation from their mother.

My next door neighbor, Jacque, and I were talking one day and she bemoaned the fact that her middle child screamed so much when she left that it was difficult to get a baby-sitter. I was working on a self-esteem project at the time, so was home a lot. Jenny (middle child) and I were friends. So, I suggested that Jacque bring Jenny over every morning and let me watch her for an hour or two. Jacque agreed.

Jenny planted herself against the front door and screamed the entire time she was here. On the second day, I was walking to the kitchen; Jenny had just begun to wane in her expressed anger. The minute she saw me, her volume went back to ear-splitting again. I squatted down and spoke into the din, "When you get tired of crying and screaming, you are welcome to come down with me. I have some records and crayons for drawing."

On the third day, a small girl with blotchy eyes and cheeks stood in my office doorway, still breathless from the previous crying attack. I looked at her, smiled, pointed to the crayons on the floor next to a coloring book and said, "If you start coloring that picture, I will join you when I am finished with my work." I reached over and switched on the record player which emitted, "Mickey Mouse" music. Jenny began to color and sing with the record.

Jacque has been extra-nice to me since this training session, so I figure she thinks there is some kind of indebtedness at hand. The truth is, crying that I understand does not bother me; I was doing my work, realizing that sooner or later, Jenny would give up her battle. Then Jacque would be able to leave without worrying about her child's pain or her own.

It is difficult not to get hooked into a small child's drama and feel guilty or be over-protective in letting go to leave. Simple words give needed information: "I am going to be gone for awhile. (Allison) is going to stay with you and take care of you. I will be back in awhile." Then the trick is to walk out and not support any drama that might occur.

For some parents, training yourself to leave your child is difficult. Learning separateness assists both you and the child in becoming inner-dependent.

KEEP BUSY HANDS BUSY

> Essential Ingredients:
> Infinite Patience • Creativity • Humor

Remember: That endlessly moving energy of your young child is curiosity on the move; curiosity needs to be nurtured and channeled, not dissolved.

The other day, a lady was trying to write a check in line while her son (about age 4) was on the move: First he put the chain up so other people couldn't get in, then he pulled out a magazine, then he got in the way of the bagger then...." The mother was fit to be tied. Having heard his name (and the word "NO") twenty seven times, I said, "Steven, look at all the cookies in that case. Which cookie would you give to the cookie monster on Sesame Street?" Steven kept busy scanning the large array of cookies, then looked back, eyes beaming and said, "This one!" The mother thanked me and staggered off with her wee pirate.

It takes forethought to do this and it can be done: Write all of your check (with credit card and driver's license number on the back) except the check amount in the car when your busy little person is contained. Give the child a continual job while in the market: Steer the cart, go get something, look for something. Talk to the child (something you can't do if you are thinking, so a detailed market list is essential). Tell your child what everything is and be willing to say it all again the next time you go to the store. **This time will pass**. The child's response to his or her own curiosity is being formed; it takes infinite patience to survive all of their energy, and your investment will be returned tenfold.

While I think children can learn to contain their energy and not continue to be explosive masses of moving motion, it seems to me that during those years from 2 to 4, especially, the quest is to channel not lessen energy.

I have seen many adults who are "dead" in terms of energy. Invariably, they were children who abounded with spontaneity and were suppressed by parents who did not understand the difference between re-routing energy and eradicating it.

Maybe, if you let yourself enjoy all that energy you will discover a part of you that was otherwise dead. Don't I know about housework and other priorities? Of course I do. I'm suggesting you change those priorities for a short period of time. Your house will survive neglect, your child(ren) will not.

ANSWERING ENDLESS QUESTIONS

> Essential Ingredients:
> Patience • Communication • Time

Remember: A questioning mind comes from curiosity and spontaneity.

All children go through a "What's that?" and "Why?" stage (usually when they are learning to talk). Some children, however, are more tenacious in their questioning.

It is easy to get impatient with a constant interruption and barrage of questions for which you may not have answers. Wanting to quiet a questioning child is a normal, natural feeling. The problem is that unanswered questions usually bring on more questions!

When I taught elementary school, it became very clear to me that knowing everything was not only unnecessary but often cut off the process where a child learns to think for him or herself. It was there I learned to explore the possibilities of where to find information rather than becoming the encyclopedia of data.

Today's child, through the media, is exposed to far more information than was true for me as a child. This awareness can set into motion questions for which answers are difficult:

A: "Mom, I saw a program where they were killing elephants. Why would people kill elephants?"

B: "They want to sell the ivory from their tusks."

A: "Why don't they just take the ivory without killing the elephants?"

B: "To get the ivory you must kill the elephant."

A: "Killing elephants is stupid! (Crying) Why don't people care about killing elephants?"

B: "Some people do. Some people are trying to protect the elephants."

A: "Well, it must not be working cuz I saw them killing them. How can we get people to stop killing elephants?"

At this point, I am out of information. My "I don't know," won't be enough information for this child's mind. Maybe the next step is to go to the library and ask for a resource concerning doing something about this problem. Children are very worried about the planet being destroyed. They want to do something about it. Apathy begets apathy. Maybe our children's concerns are a gift to all of us.

Endless questions take time. Please take time. Asking questions is a vital part of your child's development.

ACCEPTING A CHILD'S GIFT

> Essential Ingredients:
> Joy • Compassion • Gentleness

Remember: The child's heart is filled with love for you; every gift, however strange, is a statement about that love.

You will receive some incredibly interesting gifts from your children over the years. While a ceramic jeweled hand has no conceivable use to you, a child sees it as magical and wonderful...just like you.

Too often, we forget the immense value of giving and receiving something homemade. Decorating a card, a story or poem just from you, or even something like popsicle sticks all glued together are an undeniable message of love.

To this day, I have throughout our home a strange assortment of pottery and other collectables. Recently, Kathleen asked, "Why do you still have those things around. Some of them are definitely weird." I laughed and wrapped her up in my arms, "Because of the memories each one has, Kathleen. I remember this small pig-tailed girl's eyes as I opened a brown clay ashtray. It was irrelevant that no one smokes in our home. The otherwise ugly thing was made beautiful by the love surrounding it."

For my birthday one year, I opened some hand lotion and perfume from Kathleen. She told me it had taken her six weeks of saving money to buy my gifts. "Why didn't you have Dad pay for these?" I asked. Her voice was strong, "Then it would be from Dad. This present is from me."

When Kathleen graduated from high school, she gave me a necklace that she had had made just for me. It is a silver tree with hearts for leaves. I wear it whenever I give a talk. Do I love that necklace more than the brown ash tray? Yes. And I value the brown ash tray because the love which surrounds each of them is the same.

When a starry-eyed child hands you a gift which is wrapped in too much paper with too much tape...and opens to something you can't even identify...remember the love that surrounds it, and rejoice. A gift of love is always a treasure.

DISCIPLINE

MAKING AGREEMENTS

Essential Ingredients:
Communication • Listening • Follow-through

Remember: Teaching your children to make and keep agreements puts responsibility for their actions on them.

In our family, keeping your word in important. None of us break our word. Instilling this piece of integrity into my two children's lives began when they were small and continues to this day. An important step in this process is learning to make and keep agreements.

As an elementary teacher I learned that individual children hear the same thing differently. A visual learner does best when he/she sees what is to be learned, a kinesthetic learner needs to experience it, an auditory learner hears and learns. Sometimes a child does not get what you said because he or she is a different kind of "fact processor" than you. Making agreements helps give you feedback as to what was heard.

A: "Kathleen, I want you to empty the dishwasher before my meeting this morning. The meeting is at 9:00. Please tell me what you heard me say."
B: "I heard you."
A: "Nevertheless, I want to know what you heard, please.
B: You want me to empty the dishwasher before 9:00 this morning."
*A: "When do you think you might do that?"
B: "I don't know."
A: "It's 7:00 now, when do you plan to empty the dishwasher?"
B: "After this cartoon is over."
A: "I know it sounds ridiculous, but please indulge me and tell me all the parts of our agreement. "
B: "After I finish watching this cartoon, I will go and empty the dishwasher."
A: "Thank you."

The part from *A: down becomes unnecessary when you feel the child can think it through for him/herself. The point is to make a commitment to yourself about a responsibility so you are less likely to forget. If, after a reasonable amount of time has passed, the dishwasher isn't empty, simply say, "Did we make an agreement about when you would empty the dishwasher?" The child will jump into motion. If too much reminding is occurring, sit down with the child and talk about the problem, asking for his/her solution and talk about a consequence for not keeping agreements.

PRACTICE: LEARNING TO MAKE AGREEMENTS

SMALL CHILDREN:

Parent: "It's time to put all of your toys in your toy box. Let's play a game! I'll turn this timer right here (turn to appropriate number of minutes). See if you can get all of your toys into the box before you hear this sound (make the timer 'ding' and turn it back to the same amount of time). I'll watch. First tell me about your agreement — tell me what you are going to do. (Use the word "agreement" even when the child is too young to understand its meaning; it becomes a symbol for doing something you say you are going to do.) Ready....go!"

Note: Be sure to allow more time than necessary as the object of this game is to get the toys put away and have fun doing it. A positive experience is your goal.

OLDER CHILDREN

Talk about the reason for making agreements and discuss logical consequences for each agreement.

Parent: "It probably sounds silly to say something to you and then ask you to repeat it — like I think you have a dysfunctional brain. The truth is, sometimes I'm not clear when I think I'm being clear. Feedback from you tells me that we are both thinking the same thoughts."

"You need to wash the car and vacuum the interior. I'd like you to tell me what you are going to do and when you are going to do it, please."

Teen: "I'm going to wash the car, vacuum it on the inside and I will have it done by noon."

Parent: "To keep you responsible for your actions instead of me, we choose consequences for your actions. What will happen if the car is not finished by noon?"

Teen: "I don't get to drive it at all this week-end."

Parent: "High five on that agreement! Thanks."

THE CONSEQUENCE OF TYPICAL PARENT TACTICS

> Essential Ingredients:
> Awareness • Understanding • Practice

Remember: Your child's heart is made of clay — each harsh reaction imprints there for life.

Children learn to tune out a parent who scolds endlessly. Withdrawal of love tells the child that their personal value is conditional. Isolation requires a child to repress feelings or work them out alone — which may be impossible to do. Bribery teaches the child to resent power, not to be self reliant.

I've worked with many teenagers who have learned to tune out their parents lecturing. When I've said to them, "Maybe if you listened to their message, you wouldn't get so many lectures. " Their response is always the same, "There is no message except that I'm no good."

Many teenagers say they stopped talking to their parents because they got tired of hearing about how it was in the good ol' days. A quick way to invalidate feelings is to deluge your child with stories or opinions that were not requested.

People pleasers often come from an environment in which love is given and taken away, dependent upon performance. The problem with people pleasing is that one's behavior is based upon another person's response. The person who is people pleasing soon loses all sense of his/her own identity.

Bribing a child teaches that child to modify their behavior in order to get something for certain behavior. I have seen many a mother bribe a child to "be good" in the market line. That child has his/her mother over a barrel; "I will scream and embarrass you. You will bribe me. I will get a goodie. It always works."

Bribery teaches nothing except deviousness. If your child doesn't get what he/she wants and screams in the market, apologize to the people around you and ignore the screaming. Next time you go to the market, don't let that child go with you. Behavior that is not rewarded stops.

If I could isolate one gift that's made a difference in the growth and development of my two children, it is that I have loved each of them every single day since they were born. There have been days when I didn't like them, didn't want to be a parent any more...but I have loved them every minute since they were born.

PRACTICE: CONSEQUENCES OF TYPICAL PARENTAL ATTITUDES

<u>Think about the consequences of what you say before you say it:</u>

Teen: "Hey, Dad, I joined the track team today!"
Dad: "In which events?"
Teen: "Hurdles and high jump"
Dad: "I was the state champion in hurdles.I remember..."
Teen: "Gotta go...see ya!"

Feelings: *Cut off. Nothing I could do would be as good as you did. Will not accept any support given during the track season.*

Decision: **My best will not be good enough for you.**

Child: "I'd like to be a forest ranger when I get older."
Parent: "That's absurd. You don't like the mountains!"

Feelings: *Cut off. Unheard. Interpreted — not interested in who I really am.*

Decision: **Don't share any more dreams with this person.**

Child: "I want some gum!"
Parent: "No gum for you today, sorry!"
Child: (fussing) "I want some now!"
Parent: "You can get upset if you want to, and I'm not buying you any gum today."
Child: (cries and fusses)

Next Day:
Parent: "I'm going to the market. You will stay home with Daddy."
Child: "I want to go, too!"
Parent: "Sorry. Not today. Tell me why you are not going with me to the market today."
Child: "Cuz I screamed and cried yesterday."
Parent: "That's right. Screaming and yelling doesn't belong in the market. You can go with me next time."

NEVER UNDERESTIMATE THE POWER OF PEER PRESSURE

> Essential Ingredients:
> Awareness • Perseverance • Listen! Listen! Listen!

Remember: Getting along with peers is so catastrophically important to some children that they will even go against their own family to be accepted.

A survey of high school students, taken across the country, clearly indicated the effects of peer pressure. Given a chart with three easily distinguishable lines, the students were told to raise their hands when the teacher pointed to the longest line. What one student didn't know was that the rest of the class had been secretly told to raise their hand for the second longest line. Even though the directions said to vote for the longest line, the class was secretly told to vote incorrectly.

All the hands went up when the teacher pointed to the second longest line. In 75% of the situations, the "victim" looked around, saw all the hands up for what he/she thought was the wrong answer, and raised a hand anyway. That is peer pressure.

Interestingly enough, when there was one friend involved in this process, the following results occurred: Same directions were given except the teacher pointed first to the short line, then to the longest line. The class, having been told to vote for the second longest line did not raise their hands. Only one student's hand went up. The "victim" looked around, saw the one hand up, and also raised his/her hand in 78% of the cases. Point: Even one friend who will support your morals and values is essential in the process of choosing to stand up for yourself.

If, as parents, we expect our children to follow our morals and values, we must demonstrate following them, then teach our children skills so they *can* stand up for them. Morals and values are best taught through example.

If you say it is important to respect other human beings and you consistently treat others disrespectfully, you are not being consistent. As you may have noticed, all children were born with inconsistency detectors!

If you say honesty is important then brag about cheating someone (even the IRS), that moral loses value.

Preaching and moralizing are seldom valued by a child. Reading stories that involve morals, commenting on things you see or hear, and mostly sharing your thoughts about life with your children are effective ways of instilling values.

TEACHING RESPONSIBILITY

> Essential Ingredients:
> Clear Communication • Awareness • Patience

Remember: The core of teaching responsibility is to teach your child to respond to his/her environment.

Too often, a child who looks responsible is one who behaves in a certain way in order to stay out of trouble. Being responsible is responding to life around you out of a sense of caring and commitment to a certain standard of living. Teaching responsibility involves teaching with understanding and following through on consequences.

As a child, the answer to why something needed to be done was, "Because I said so!" That is the way parents of my generation taught. Today, I think there is great value in using words that give meaning to each direction you give:

"The living room rug has chips on it and needs to be vacuumed before the little pieces grind into the carpet."

"Your toys need to be put back into your toybox so we have a safe place to walk."

"We keep our jackets in closets. If all of us put our jackets on the floor, it wouldn't be safe to walk."

"I don't want our home to look like a dump, please put your trash into the trash can."

"Glasses that need to be washed go on the sink in the kitchen. That way, you know where it is when you get thirsty again. Also, we can wash it if you are finished using it."

"I can see that you are very upset, and you cannot throw or try to break things in the house when you are angry."

Teaching children to be responsible for their feelings is as important as being responsible for their actions. The primary requirement in teaching each area is:

Feelings: Honor as valuable, any feeling. Don't try to squash or have the child disown feelings. Be a safe place where children can express their feelings and get assistance in channeling them into appropriate behavior.

Actions: Use consequences instead of punishment. Be as consistent as possible in your requirements and follow-through. Communicate! Communicate! Communicate!

DISTINGUISH THE DIFFERENCE BETWEEN
PUNISHMENT AND CONSEQUENCES

Essential Ingredients:
Separate Child/Action • Love Your Child • Patience

Remember: Punishment turns the parent into a warden and invites resentment; consequences are a natural part of life.

Mistakes are the way we learn. I know no one who is exempt from making mistakes. Naturally, one tries to avoid making mistakes, but they do happen.

When mistakes are regarded as CATASTROPHIC events with a huge drama created around them, the spontaneity of children is dissipated. If you are afraid to make a mistake or afraid you'll get into trouble, you withhold. Some caution is of value, however it is essential to give children permission to learn and grow from their mistakes.

Punishment by its very term says to the child, "You did it wrong and I am going to get even with you." Where is the learning in that? If they change their behavior is it because they want you off their back or because they really learned that it was inappropriate behavior? Ask the colleges what happens when "good little boys and girls" who have been pleasing their parents get turned loose for the first time. Some of them take their hostility out on the whole school.

A consequence is a natural result of an action. If I drive too fast and get a ticket, the ticket is a consequence of my choice. If I forget to put the meat out, everyone gets to participate in my consequence at dinner that night.

Be certain the consequence matches the problem. I see no relationship to taking away television time because your child left his/her bicycle out overnight. Take the bicycle away for a day. A day, not two months is appropriate.

It is wise not to state consequences when you are angry. "You will never ride that bicycle to school again!" isn't a consequence, its a punishment and — chances are it is a threat you won't keep. Say instead, "I need to think about the consequence of your actions. We'll talk about it later."

Consequences teach children about life. If you protect your children from their consequences, they will have some enormous shocks as they get older. Don't make cripples out of children who will otherwise learn to walk. Consequences are great teachers.

GIVE CONSEQUENCES WITHOUT EMOTION

> Essential Ingredients:
> Patience • Awareness • Practice

Remember: A child cannot hear your message through his/her fear of your anger.

When a child does something that requires a consequence, it may be difficult to administer it calmly without anger. Don't give a consequence when you are angry. First of all, you will tend to over-react and give too big a consequence. Also, your child will misinterpret the action as being revenge rather than a logical consequence.

If you are angry say, "I am really upset about this. I want you to sit in that chair until I tell you to move. I will talk about your consequence in a few minutes."

My mother doesn't think you will understand that you did something wrong unless she wraps her message in lots of anger. She frowns, presents all sorts of negative body language, and barks out the message. My children, who are used to some sort of communication about a problem ask, "Why did 'Gee-Gee' get so angry about that little thing?"

My job is not to make grandma wrong, it is to teach. So I said, "That's the way your grandmother talks." If the children asked, "Why doesn't she use friendly words?" I responded, "Maybe she doesn't know how to do that."

No two family members handle their anger the same way. A child will be exposed to all sorts of angry responses in their life. It is important to teach the concept that "That's just the way they are" rather than to label the person as being deficient in some way.

My father had a basic strategy for parenting that I have found invaluable: **REPRIMAND BEHIND THE BARN AND PRAISE FROM THE ROOFTOPS.**

The whole family does not need to be in on the consequence unless the whole family is responsible for the consequence. If one child asks, "Why is Kathleen walking to school each day?" say, "Kathleen forgot to bring her bicycle inside one night, so she cannot ride her bike to school for three days." Simple question, simple answer.

Though anger is a natural response to life and needs to be expressed appropriately, it is not a motivator for improvement. Your job is to teach your child skills for life.

COMMUNICATION WITH CONSEQUENCES

> Essential Ingredients:
> Clarity • Follow Through • Kindness

Remember: Consequences are the natural result of an action, punishment is perceived as getting even.

Let's say, your son continues to take tools from the tool chest and leaves them all over the place. There have been endless promises to do it differently. You find a rusty pair of pliers in the yard, and that is the last straw.

A: "I found these pliers in the back yard. It belongs in the tool box. (Stating your want) I want tools put back into the tool box."

B: "I'm sorry Dad, I won't forget again."

A: "Some steel wool and elbow grease will fix it. I will show you how to clean it, then we will talk some more. "(consequence)

B: "Look, Dad! The pliers are all fixed. What is that?"

A: "I put a lock on the tool box. You will need to ask me for something before you use it from now on." (consequence)

B: "But Dad, what if you are at work?"

A: "Sorry, son. The tools need to be in the tool box. When I feel you will keep that rule, we will talk about taking the lock off the box." (In an appropriate amount of time, remove the lock, talk about the consequences if tools are left out, and prepare to follow through again if necessary.)

Your child is asked to pick up the toys in the living room, but somehow escapes to play before doing so. **"Forgetting" is getting to be a habit.** The following words state the problem and the consequence:

A: "I asked you to pick up your toys before you went out to play." (the problem)

B: "Oh, yea! Sorry Mom, I'll do it now!"

A: "I picked them up for you. I have put them into a bag and will keep them for two days." (consequence)

B: "But Mom, my baseball was on the floor!"

A: "Sorry, Son. If someone does your job for you it might not get done the way you want it to be done. Next time, if you choose to do what is asked of you, you will have your baseball. " (consequence)

B: "Mom, I promise I will pick up my messes right away."

A: "I'm sure you will....next time."

COMMUNICATION WITH CONSEQUENCES #2

> Essential Ingredients:
> Listening • Patience • Follow-through

Remember: You are training your child to be self-motivated, not to react out of fear of you.

Tyrant techniques look like they work because the child responds instantly. However, feelings of anger, resentment, revenge can build, eventually leading to behavior which is destructive. Teaching a child to react to you out of fear does not teach the child self-motivation in his or her choices. Your job is to teach your children to think about the results of their choices and actions—not what to do in order to keep you off their back.

The following conversation is straight-forward, honest, instructive and a requirement for change:

"I have a problem with the mess in the living room and I want you to go in and clean it up right now. All of your toys are to be put away in your toy box, not thrown on the floor in your bedroom. Any questions?"

A harsh tone of voice, hostile gestures, and little words added here and there, turn a clear concise message into one which can damage self-esteem. Choose your words wisely:

"You came in at 12:45 last night. Your curfew is 12:00. Since you don't have any reason for being so late, you will be in tonight at 11:15." (To teach my children to respect time, I took a minute off their curfew time for every minute they were late. Repeated infractions warranted moving to five minutes for every minute late.) I think it's important to trust your instincts on listening to excuses; I've been late more than once because of unexpected traffic. There is a difference between a logical reason and an excuse.

Rules cannot be enforced with consequences unless your children know exactly what rules you have. **Be sure you are clear in communicating what you want from your children** so that consequences become a natural result of choice.

A: "What is our rule about curfew?"
B: "In by 12:00."
A: "What time did you get in last night?"
B: "Quarter to one."
A: "And what time will you be in tonight as a result of last night's choice?"
B: "Mom!"
A: "What time, please."
B: "Eleven fifteen."
A: "Eleven fifteen sharp. Any questions?"

TEACHING RESPONSIBILITY AND CONSEQUENCES

> Essential Ingredients:
> Trust • Patience • Clear Communication

Remember: Your job is to teach your child to be inner-dependent.

An entry from my journal when Scott was nine reads: "Yesterday after the children went to school, I discovered Scott had forgotten his lunch. My instinct was to go over to school and drop it off for him. Then I asked myself what he would learn from that — that good ol' Mom would bail him out when he doesn't take care of himself. So I put the lunch on his bed. When he got home from school and saw the lunch, he was angry saying, 'Why didn't you bring my lunch? I was starving!' I responded, 'If you depend upon me to take care of you I'll have to do it your whole life, and that wouldn't be good for either one of us. You may be as upset with me if you wish. The fact is *you* forgot your lunch.' The next morning Scott bounced out of the door, leaned back in with that wonderful grin saying, 'Hey Mom, got my lunch!'"

The easiest thing in the world to do is to rescue your children from their own choices. It is unreasonable to think you will NEVER do so, and caution is recommended.

The difficulty in so many of the parenting choices is finding the middle ground. I think too severe a consequence is as damaging as none. For me, a constant consideration is what lesson is to be learned and is he/she getting the message? It is difficult to consider those thoughts while angry, so setting consequences is best done with a rational mind.

Involving the child in choosing a consequence is often a valuable lesson in itself. A child filled with remorse can suggest far too severe a consequence, so negotiating is important. The questions to be asked are:

1. What was the problem? (What happened is the story, the problem is the core of the issue) Example: I left my bicycle outside overnight.

2. How is that a problem? Example: It could have gotten stolen.

3. What is your responsibility towards the bicycle? Example: To put it away.

4. What could we do to help you remember your responsibility? Example: Not let me ride the bike for two days. (Be sure to enforce the two days with no negotiating.)

HANDLING YOUR OWN GUILT

> Essential Ingredients:
> Resolve • Understanding • Patience

Remember: You are teaching your child the necessary skills in order to survive in a very harsh world; you cannot always be best friends and accomplish this task.

When your child goes to elementary school, you will hear (especially with the girls) a phrase that sounds something like this, "If you do this with me, I will be your best friend."

Probably in the book all children seem to have read prior to birth, your children read and understand that one of the places you might be willing to compromise is tied up with having them like you. Even if you are able to calmly decide that being angry with you is rational behavior for a child who isn't getting what he/she wants, there is a tendency to compromise in order to get your friendly relationship back.

Another feeling which borders on irrationality is to feel guilty when you force your child to stop doing something that is fun and accomplish some task. The level of difficulty in this game increases substantially when your child is a teenager, as the unwilling participant will supply ample moans, groans and frowning looks to accompany your wish. Bottom line: all of life isn't fun. It is essential we as parents teach our children to interrupt fun in order to do what needs to be done.

A parent needs to come to terms with the fact that if there were a choice to be made, you would choose having your child's respect over their friendship. A child cannot take your friendship out into the world (except as emotional support); he/she will take whatever you are willing to stand up for in terms of training. "How much do I want my child to feel and be safe in an unsafe world?" may be the question you need to ask yourself whenever you feel guilty for being strict. And, for the sake of your mind which may be wanting to rant and rave right now, my considerable experience with teenagers clearly indicates that the children who have been strongly guided both respect and love their parents to a far greater degree than children from permissive homes.

"If I follow this line of behavior, what will I be teaching my child?" is a painful yet powerful question to ask yourself from time-to-time. And...it isn't easy to do "the right thing" when you love your child so much, wanting to be loved in return. Just remember: every choice has a consequence. Whenever possible, make choices which teach your child to be self-reliant.

DON'T THREATEN YOUR CHILDREN

> Essential Ingredients:
> Self-discipline • Patience • Understanding

Remember: When you threaten a child you initiate a challenge rather than teach a lesson.

There is so much to learn as a young child, so many people to try to please. To me, all of life is a matter of attitude and perspective. If you perceive your child as a little monster who is trying to drive you crazy, you will treat that child differently than if you see him/her as a tiny human who needs lots of coaching.

Many adults use threatening techniques with children because they look like they work. In fact, they do not. First of all, threats are tiring. As a parent you need to remember who you threatened with what, and if you want to maintain your status as a power monger, you need to keep all the threats you make.

Secondly, a threat isn't respectful of the possibility that your child might want to get along with you and is capable of solving each problem. Do you say to your best friend, "If you are late picking me up to go shopping I won't ever talk to you again!?" No. Why? It's insulting to be treated that way.

Put a tape recorder on in the room during dinner. Listen to yourself for one day. Watch how you talk, especially when you are angry. Every time you threaten your child, you put another brick in the wall between the two of you.

The object is to teach your children to be inner-dependent. Look at that word again: **inner-dependent**, which is to say, to make appropriate choices for themselves so they live productive, useful lives. If you become a policeman and then a warden, all you do is teach your children to resent power.

There is no question with either of my children as to who is the boss. When I ask something is to be done, it gets done. I am not supportive of letting children rule a house. It is easy to threaten children because working things out through communication is something few of us know much about. What I offer for your consideration is my belief that threatening your children will cause more problems than solutions.

PRACTICE: LEARNING NOT TO THREATEN YOUR CHILD

After repeated conversation about cleaning up a mess:

No: "If you don't clean up this mess right now, you will not go to the dance this week-end!"

Yes: "Enough is enough. Right now. No arguments. No exceptions. This mess is to be picked up before dinner; that's one hour. Until this mess is picked up satisfactorily, you are to stay in this room. Any questions?"

Note: Once your children are trained that *now* means *now*, these little dramas will become unnecessary.

When you walk into the room, Peggy is hitting Joey:

No: "If you hit your brother again, I'm going to spank you!"

Yes: "Listen to me! You are not to hit Joey. Use your words, not your fists. I'm putting you into the dining room for ten minutes so you will both cool off. If you hit Joey again, you will be back in the dining room for a longer time. Do you understand?"

Note: Who started the fight is irrelevant. A consequence of hitting someone is that you might be the only one caught doing the hitting. Joey may need to be reminded to use his words, not his fists. If both children are caught fighting, send both to a "penalty box" for ten minutes. Why the dining room? Nothing fun is happening in the dining room.

INFLICTING GUILT IS HARMFUL

Essential Ingredients:
Compassion • Understanding • Patience

Remember: The little things you say are taken into the heart of your child and registered there forever.

When your small tots are running you ragged, to threaten, yell and inflict guilt seem like natural self-defense measures. When a technique works, a parent tends to adopt that mode of relating to the child all the time. What is difficult to see is that what works on the surface may be destructive in the long run.

As infants your children are like sponges, taking in every idea, every message and holding it as their own. Their sense of self-esteem is molded by your perception of them. Each message from you is logged and carefully acknowledged. If you think of yourself as a coach in a continual process of teaching and carefully choose the words for each message you send, you will give your children their needed coaching without doing any harm.

"You made me ruin dinner tonight!" might seem like an innocent enough statement, but inflicted guilt is always received with anger. In addition the rest of the family may add fuel to the fire with their own resentment. Group coercion seldom teaches responsibility and self-reliance. Such pressure creates an increasing sense of alienation and resentment that often manifests itself in rebellion and low self-esteem.

At age five, one of my friend's father told her that her mother had miscarried because she was such a bad girl. At forty, this friend is still trying to untie herself from the web those words cast around her heart.

Guilt is destructive. If you make a mistake, feeling badly is natural. Nevertheless, one's energy needs to move to correcting either the situation or the behavior that caused the situation. A conversation about how you might do something differently if it happened again is far more valuable than being sent to your room to think about the awful thing you did. Research indicates that when a child is banished, he/she does everything but think about his/her responsibility in that action.

Inflicting guilt is harmful and not constructive to the development of a caring, compassionate human-in-the-making.

PRACTICE: NOT USING GUILT TO MOTIVATE CHILDREN

No: "You made your sister angry."

Yes: "Your sister is angry. I want you two to use your words to work out your problem."

Note: No one makes anyone angry. Telling Robin she has the power to make Barbara angry is giving Robin a weapon. No one controls another person's emotions.

No: "Your mother went to bed. She says she's exhausted because you were such a bad girl today."

Yes: "Your mother has gone to bed. She says you two had a long hard day. "

Note: Whether to seek the child's version or not is a choice. It is not advisable to become the middle person for two people's conflict. Stop any complaining with, "You and your mother need to work out your problems. Maybe you could talk to her about your feelings tomorrow."

Use your instinct as to whether your child needs to be heard or not.

No: "You've given me a headache!"

Yes: "My head aches so I need you to get a book and read quietly for awhile."

GETTING YOUR CHILD TO MIND YOU

> Essential Ingredients:
> Patience • Follow Through • Kindness

Remember: Children need a warning in order to gracefully switch activities.

Your child is in the swimming pool and it is time to go home, so you say, "Kathleen, it's time to go!" While you get busy picking up the towels and mess, Kathleen disappears under water (great strategy as one cannot hear under water). You give another reminder: "Kathleen, it's time to go!" And this time the child gives you a standard stalling reply, "Just one more..." After a few minutes of repeated calls, you lose your cool and go charging across the cement to either scream at your little darling or haul him/her out of the pool and scream. All of this behavior is tiring, embarrassing and a huge space invasion for the people around you.

Instead: Five minutes before you are ready to go, go over to your child and say. "I can see you are having a wonderful time. It is time for us to go home. In five minutes, you will get out of the pool and we will leave. I will tell you when there is one minute left, then I want you to come right away."

What if he/she doesn't come? Be willing to back up that what you say is what you mean. Go over to your child and say firmly, "Time is up, we are going to go. Please come out, now." Interrupt any plea bargaining with a firm, "Now, please." If your child should dive under the water and swim away ask the lifeguard to help you or simply walk into the pool and carry the child out. The drama will only occur as long as there is doubt in the child's mind that you mean business. After that, "Now!" will mean "Now!"

Some children seem to resist going to bed at night. Having your child go to bed is for their health and for your right to have some time without that child. It usually works best if you give some warning that the time for them to be alone is coming: "When this program is over, it will be your bed time," lets the child know what is to follow. Reading to a child helps them calm down, relax and let go of being with you for this day. If a child comes back out after being put to bed, simply return him/her to bed saying, "This is your bed time. If you want to read a book you may do that. You may not come out with Daddy and me because this is our time to be together." Persistence may be quelled with a gate. When a child realizes that his/her persistence will not pay off, the behavior will stop.

MAKE YOUR "NOS" COUNT

> Essential Ingredients:
> Determination • Perseverance • Trust

Remember: Even though children fight boundaries, they need them as guidelines for living.

If you have toddlers, you might take a counter and see how many times in a day you say the word, "No". Chances are, the number will be staggering.

When children hear something over and over one of two things happen: (1) They learn to react not to respond, or (2) They learn to turn a deaf ear to it.

It is advisable to use the word "No" sparingly. "Don't touch that, it's hot!" tells the child to avoid the hot dish and saves a no for later.

Take a child firmly away from another child if a fight is in progress, saying, "We use our words not our fists in this house. You are not to hit Matthew!" (And I think hitting your child for hitting another child is absurd!)

With older children, gather all the data about their request before you make your decision. To the question, "Mom, can I go to the show with Robin?" you might quickly respond, "No." Then, being given the information that parents are going, the hour is good and that they want to treat your child, you might say, "OK, then you can go!" You took back a "No".

When your child asks you to do something say, "I don't have enough information to make a responsible decision. Tell me more of the details." If you always respond this way to a request, your children will learn to give you information up-front. Then you might hear, "Mom, Robin asked me to go to the show. Her whole family is going, and they are treating. We will go at 7:00 and be home by 9:30. I'd really like to go."

Say *no* when you really want to say *no*. When you say *no*, mean it and do not take it back. When *no* means *no* to a teenager, a time of huge power struggles can be diminished. (See page 132 for the Broken Record, a holding-the-line skill).

SENDING CHILDREN TO THEIR ROOM
CAN CAUSE EMOTIONAL DAMAGE

> Essential Ingredients:
> Patience • Awareness • Kindness

Remember: When a small child is sent to his/her room to think about what they have done, the best they can do is to think about how mean you are.

Sometimes, when tempers fly, it is in the best interest of the child to send him/her to a quiet place. Sending a child to his/her room to cool off (or until you cool off) is a different message than being sent into isolation to do penance.

Most of us have enormous amounts of fear concerning abandonment and rejection. Fear causes the part of the brain that reasons to shut down, so a child literally cannot sit and think about what he/she has done wrong.

Abandonment and rejection cause anger and in some children, rage. To be rejected because you didn't do something right is not an incentive to do better. Even though some children will actually do better to get that parent off of their back, what goes underground is anger, resentment and too often, revenge.

Doing things to stay out of trouble is learning to manipulate people, rather than learning to use appropriate behavior. People pleasing comes from trying to win someone's love. Communication and consequences teach without harm.

If you need to be separated from your child, send him/her to the dining room. Nothing is happening in the dining room. There are no toys in the dining room. "Please go sit in the dining room until I come and talk to you," is a consequence any child will notice.

Please think about how much it hurt you if one of your parents banished you for negative behavior. To be angry with the child's behavior is a far different message from being angry with the child. If you use rejection as the means of control there will be very high premiums in the years ahead. In a world filled with "enemies" and people who abuse each other, make your home a safe place to learn from mistakes.

SPANKING A CHILD IS UNNECESSARY

> Necessary Ingredients:
> A Firm Resolve • Self-control • Patience

Remember: We live in a very violent society. Hitting is associated with intent to harm. It misrepresents the effort which is to correct behavior.

In my travels teaching workshops on parenting, I always get the question, "Do you believe in spanking as a means of correction?" I do not.

To me, spanking convinces the child that power is important, and power over someone requires violence. The four things I've seen spanking teach are: Fear, deviousness, lying and aggression.

If your child hits another child, and you hit your child using these words, "You are not to hit your friends!" What message have you really given?

Hitting a child says, I'll teach you not to do this again!" The child adds to your message, "..around me!" An angry wounded child is not likely to consider that his/her action had a consequence. (Spanking is not a consequence, it is a punishment).

Instead, take the child who hit his/her friend and put that child across the room. "You need to use your words, not your fists. When you can play with (Doug) without hitting, you may come back into this part of the room." If the child comes back, get up, walk him/her back to the original spot and say, "Stay here until I tell you to come back." **Remember: Your child is in training and is checking out if you mean what you say. If you stick to your guns now, your parenting will get progressively easier.**

It is easy, when rage sets in, to want to hit the child. I have wanted to strangle each of my children many times. I made a promise to myself never to hit either child. I have not always kept that promise. And that promise has been put to a test many times. What I've found is that hitting children is unnecessary. Right? Wrong? I don't have a way of knowing that — except it is wrong for me. What I've learned in nineteen years of parenting, is that hitting is not necessary.

By the way, I use the punching bag in the garage when my emotions are out-of-hand. The punching bag has nothing to learn, my children do. The punching bag cannot be physically or emotionally harmed, my children can be.

OVER-PERMISSIVENESS IS HARMFUL

> Essential Ingredients:
> Determination • Over-permissiveness • Awareness

Remember: Your job is not to be your child's buddy. If an action causes you to wonder whether your child will regard you with respect or friendship, choose respect.

Studies have indicated that more disturbed children come from over-permissive homes than from authoritarian homes.

Children from over-permissive homes tend to be demanding, self-centered and unable to consider the rights of others.

From my work in drug abuse , I learned that the child quickly defines over-permissiveness as a lack of caring for them. I remember talking to a twelve year old boy who said, "My folks? They don't give a damn." I asked, "How do you know?" to which he replied, "They never told me they would break my neck if I didn't get off of drugs. They don't care what I do to myself."

Recently, I asked Scott, "How come you haven't gotten into drugs?" After giving me his famous **"Are you from outer space?"** look, he said, "Because my mother would take a baseball bat and beat the (blank) out of me. Then she would drag my half-dead body out to the driveway and drive the car back and forth over my body."   I laughed saying, "Good reason!"   I don't hit my children. Scott was saying that he wouldn't because he wouldn't. And I would create hell on earth for him if he did. He's right. For me, it is a spiritual commitment to keep my mind clear and take full responsibility for my actions. You can't do that on drugs.

Talking to a child so he/she understands what is going on is not permissive. Giving reasonable, rational consequences for behavior is not permissive. Separating a child from his or her actions is not permissive. Venting anger in an appropriate manner and talking to the child in a responsible way, is not permissive. Loving your child every single day is not permissive.

Permissive behavior is passive behavior. Instead of doing something wrong, the permissive person fails to act at all. Taking time to explain things to your child, correcting behavior and loving the child, working with anger and all the day-to-day stresses of being a parent are not passive. It takes far more energy to be a teacher than a dictator. The pay-off comes in the results — and there are no replays in the end.

KEEPING THEIR ROOM CLEAN

> Essential Ingredients:
> Patience • Consistency • Consequences

Remember: In the whole list of things you want your children to be and do, keeping their rooms neat may not be a priority item.

In high school, Scott got an "A" on an English paper entitled, "Why Kids Should Be Allowed to Keep Their Rooms Messy." His primary point (and the point most teenagers will make) is that they are controlled in every single area of their life. Their room is the only place that is really theirs. All teenagers feel they should have one place that is theirs and theirs alone.

So, where do you draw the line? I don't know. Over the years, I have changed my policy so many times that I'd be lying if I called myself an authority in this area. Primarily, I have left Scott and his room alone.

Once in awhile, I say, "I know you want to control the quality of cleanliness of your room, and I'm mostly willing to concede on that item. However, it is time to reinstate some sort of civilized order. I want the floor entirely clean and vacuumed, your desk cleared off, and your closet clean. Please get rid of clothes that no longer fit. You have until Sunday to accomplish this goal. After Sunday I will go in there and will not be held responsible for what is thrown away or rearranged. Agreed?" With as little side-coaching as to details, Scott manages to reinstate some order to his pit.

Kathleen got interested in neatness around fifteen. (I waited for the same bug to bite Scott, but to no avail.) She redecorated her room and tends to be self-motivated in keeping her room quite orderly. He? Well, there's still hope!

If you are building a room for a child, I recommend walk-in closets. Scott wears XL everything and there is no way those huge clothes fit in his closet space. Kathleen tosses unironed clothes on her walk-in closet floor, and gets to them when she needs them.

For most children, the state of their room becomes a major power struggle with their parents. With so many other challenges in the offering, I have chosen to let this issue go. It has worked out fine; I never go into Scott's bedroom so it doesn't bother me that his pit is the pittiest pit I have ever seen. His grandmother went into his bedroom once — her heart has been beating faster ever since, and she has wisely chosen not to repeat that act.

HANDLING TATTLING

Essential Ingredients:
Communication • Consistency • Patience

Remember: The child tattles to get you involved in his or her problem — which is not good for the child.

There is a wonderful lesson in the book, **Project Self-Esteem** on handling tattling. I will overview the dynamics of tattling for you, here:

- Reporting has to do with safety.

- When someone tattles, he/she has a stake in the outcome.

If one of your children wraps a vegetable up in the napkin and the other child tells you about it, is that tattling or reporting? Since no safety is involved, it is minding someone else's business which is tattling.

One child gets under the kitchen sink and is pouring liquid soap all over the floor. The other child runs to get you. Tattling or reporting? Since safety is involved, it is reporting.

From second grade on, your child is capable of understanding this concept. Once the "rules" are determined, all you have to do is ask a question when a child comes up to you to tattle: "Melody, are you tattling or reporting?" If the child says, "Yes, but...", simply repeat your question.

Children tattle for a variety of reasons: revenge, jealousy, recognition, helplessness, or to elevate self. Tattling is minding someone else's business. It needs to stop. You stop it by simply asking a question and refusing to participate in the "Yes, but..." game.

Child: "Jason took the kleenex out of the bathroom."

Parent: (...asking yourself if safety is involved) "Are you tattling or reporting?"

Child: "The kleenex is aspose to be in the bathroom."

Parent: "Are you tattling or reporting?"

Child: "You don't even care about the kleenex!"

Parent: "Tattling or reporting?"

Child: "Oh, never mind!"

If only all of the parenting skills could be so easy!

HANDLING TEASING

> Essential Ingredients:
> Trust • Patience • Perseverance

Remember: Children who tease only tease those who respond in some way.

A frequent concern of parents is working with a child who is being teased. It is a natural reaction to want to protect our children from hurt or harm. Our job however, is to teach our children to protect themselves.

The reason people tease: To get even, out of jealousy, to make someone notice you and because that person does not feel good about him/herself.

Trying to change other people does not work. It isn't your business to change others. Changing your response to others is not always an easy task.

While doing the research for Project Self-Esteem, we taught children in a variety of schools to simply **think** this phrase when they were being teased: "No matter what you say or do I'm still a worthwhile person." We were amazed at how high a percentage of children who had been troubled by teasing, ceased to have the problem with no other intervention. (Note: A child is to *think* not *say* that phrase.)

With some students, using the broken record (see pg. 132) and saying, "I don't like it when you tease me and I want you to stop," will stop the behavior.

A person who teases seems to thrive on abusing others. It is also important to point out to your children that teasing (which seems like fun because everyone is laughing) may harm another person. The two methods above have had remarkable success wherever they have been used.

When Scott was in fourth grade, someone dubbed him "Dumbo" because he had big ears. Truth is, he was big all over, but the focus got onto his ears. Unfortunately, I did not know the two methods stated above at that time. I watched helplessly as Scott let his hair grow long to cover his ears, always wore a baseball cap and suffered from the teasing. My feeble attempts to mollify his hurt with such facts as, "Well, they don't have much to tease you about if they are picking on your ears," fell onto (no pun intended) deaf ears. Eventually, he gave up his concern, returning to a flat-top (thank goodness!).

Children must learn not to be a victim to other people's lack of kindness. It is not an easy thing for children (or adults) to learn.

FIGHTING

Essential Ingredients: Communication • Determination • Consistency

**Remember: Children fight because they feel helpless
and because they want to keep their parents involved.**

You are driving down the road and suddenly war breaks out in
the back of the car. It has been statistically proven that you can't drive a
car safely and break up a war-zone. What to do? Pull over and stop the
car. Turn off car and the radio. Sit there. When asked, "Why did you stop,
Mom?" simply reply, "It is not safe for me to drive when people are fighting in the car. I will not drive this car when there is fighting."

Whether you are going somewhere you need to be or somewhere
the children want to be, waiting works. If necessary, rearrange the seating
order to reroute any effort to resume the battle.

If your children start fighting in the market line, firmly separate
them with these words: "You may not fight in the market." Put one child
in front of you the other behind you and do not allow any poking or jab-
bing around you.

One time, I was in a clothes store looking for a gift. Kathleen and
Scott began duking it out. I separated them and said in my stern mother-
ly voice, "You may not fight in this store!" They looked at me, at each
other, walked straight through the store, out in front of the big glass win-
dows and resumed their punching match. They were five and seven
years old. I laughed (what else could I do?), and resumed shopping.
When one came up to me crying about being hurt by a punch I said, "I'm
sorry you are hurt. When you learn to use your words instead of your
fists you won't hurt each other."

My two children will chase each other all over the house teasing,
but they stopped fighting somewhere around Kindergarten and second
grade.

When Kathleen gets Scott's goat today, he (at 6'4") can pick her up
and put her outside the door. What I notice is how gentle he is with her;
they learned to use their words so they don't hurt each other physically
any more.

STEALING

> Essential Ingredients:
> Communication • Follow-through • Compassion

Remember: How you handle stealing molds a child's self-esteem and sense of morality.

Kathleen was 8 and Scott was 6 when I noticed the two of them playing happily with an assortment of stickers. "Those are great stickers!" I said, sitting on the floor, "I bet they cost someone a lot of money." Guilty looks prevailed. Asking if they stole the stickers would be stating the obvious, so I said, "I don't remember paying for these, so I have a concern that you two took them from the store. It is hard to tell the truth in a time like this, and I'd like to hear the truth." Indeed, they had taken them.

I told my frightened little elves that the people who owned the store had bought the stickers. When they took them, those people wouldn't have the money they needed to take care of their children, their home and themselves. Stealing hurts people and as they knew well by this time, I have a problem with hurting people.

Kathleen and Scott were told that they needed to go and tell the store owners what they had done; two very frightened children went to get their jackets. Meanwhile, I called the store saying, "Two darling children are about to come into your store to tell you they stole some stickers. They will give you some money they borrowed from me to pay for the stickers. I don't want you to be harsh, and I want you to help me impress on my two kids that they are not to steal."

It was very quiet on our drive to the store. When we arrived, Kathleen asked, "Aren't you going in with us?" I responded in an even tone, "I didn't steal the stickers, you did; you need to go and tell the people what happened and how you feel about it." It was also very quiet on the way home from the store.

When we got home, we made a list of chores they would do in the next few days in order to pay me for the stickers. A couple of days later, we sat down and talked about what had happened, how they had felt and what they had learned.

I didn't punish the children further as walking in that store alone seemed to impress them.

EAT EVERYTHING ON YOUR PLATE OR NO DESSERT

> Essential Ingredients:
> Patience • Insight • Communication

**Remember: Children are in different growth patterns —
sometimes they need more/less food than others.**

As the mother it is difficult to realize how many decisions you make about what everybody is going to eat each day. That can be a very tiresome role, especially when your choices are met with endless disapproval.

I'm in my late 40's, and almost everyone my age jokes about cleaning your plate because of "the starving people in China". At our dinner table you had to eat something of everything and it was a rule that you clean your plate.

My son, Scott has taught me a lot about feeding children. Sometimes, on a Saturday, I will ask him if he has eaten breakfast (or maybe even lunch). If he says, "No" I move right into my "starving child" syndrome and resort to asking, "Why not?" In his most patient tone, he will reply, "I only eat when I am hungry, don't you?"

There's a difference between teenagers who can take care of their own needs and little tots who need tending. However, I found life got a lot easier when I'd ask a simple question like, "Are you getting hungry?" If the answer were affirmative, I might offer a choice of menu: "Would you rather have a sandwich, soup or maybe a half-sandwich and a cup of soup?"

At dinner, I always put the meal onto plates and bowls from which each member can serve him/herself. My request is that each person takes at least one bite of everything, and I do not get attached to how much food any one person takes. I absolutely hate lima beans. If those ghastly things are ever served on my dinner table, I'd be the last one to eat them. Everyone has preferences — and what I've found is that children's interests in food can change dramatically over the years. Kathleen, who had a major trauma over eating almost any vegetable as a child, now joins me in eating a mostly vegetarian diet. Scott, who would reject meat as a baby, still prefers pasta and raw vegetables. Both of my children are extremely healthy and tend to self-regulate the quantity of their sugar intake.

If you serve fruit and other healthful items for dessert, the power struggle over how much dinner needs to be eaten before you get dessert is eliminated.

RESPECT

RESPECT ISN'T SOMETHING YOU GIVE, IT'S SOMETHING YOU ARE

> Essential Ingredients:
> Patience • Kindness • Listen to Your Words

Remember: You teach respect most by modeling.

Respect is best taught within the framework of the family. If one parent talks against the other parent behind his or her back, it forces the children to take sides and diminishes respect for both parents.

Respecting space is a vital issue and simply means that each member of the family has the right to have some time to him/herself.

How you talk to your children is either respectful or not. How they talk to you is either respectful or not. I think respect is far less a matter of "yes sir, no sir" type behavior and more a case of whether or not respect is given, person-to-person. Words and tone of voice are indicators of respect being spoken, not necessarily of respect being given. I don't put restrictions on what my children say, and I do ask them to do a "replay" if their tone of voice bothers me. Mainly, I treat each child with respect.

Would you say to your husband at dinner, "Sit up straight and chew with your mouth closed!?"

Would your husband smack the back of your hand at the magazine rack saying, "Don't touch anything!?"

Would you say to your best friend, "Are you going to wear that awful shirt again today?"

Would you call your friend, "Stupid" or "Dummy" or "Lazy" or "Clumsy" or "(censored)?"

A child is a tiny human with feelings, needs and lots of questions to be answered. If you respect how difficult it is to be a child in a world of so much turmoil, then treating your children with the respect they deserve is easy.

I'm not suggesting you don't get angry or have needs of your own. I am saying that every single thing you say to your child is an investment in his or her emotional stability. Children who are treated with respect generally mirror that behavior with their friends and especially their family.

TEACHING CHILDREN TO RESPECT AND VALUE
TIME FOR THEMSELVES

> Essential Ingredients:
> Model it! • Communication • Individual Respect

Remember: Parents who take time for themselves teach the value of self-care.

Though most of us are unaware that such a commodity exists, everyone needs space and time for themselves. Some people need it more than others. My daughter, Kathleen has learned to say,"I came home early to give myself some space. I'm going to read for awhile." The important thing for me to do is to honor that need and leave her alone. Everything I want to talk to her about will wait, When she is overwhelmed, she can't hear what I have to say, anyway.

When I close the door to my office it is a signal not to interrupt. Both of my children honor that signal. If one of them knocks or enters the room, I don't need to holler or scream. "Not now, please. Close the door behind you" are the only words that child needs to hear. Later, a discussion about what happened gives information to fill in those spots where there could be hurt feelings. I explain that just seeing them tells me a need exists. It is unnecessary for me to say, "I will talk to you when I can." Too many spoken words break my train of thought (which is why I closed the door). The exception to this rule occurs when there is an emergency.

Sometimes, I will sit out in the back yard in the late evening or even at night. One of my children might ask, "You OK?" to which I respond, "I'm fine, thank you, I'm just taking some time for myself."

You teach most by what you model. Modeling the right to have time for yourself is a vital ingredient for your child in a world that is much-too-mental, and where all possible space is filled with recorded sound.

For years, my children have seen me go out the door in the early morning for my walk. The only criteria I have on those walks is to appreciate what I see. I do not think about the day ahead, problems or anything else. It is a spiritual time of valuing my life. Time taken for me gives me more to give — and again, it is modeling that taking space is valuable.

SPEAKING FEELINGS MEANS BEING ABLE TO TELL THE TRUTH

> Essential Ingredients:
> Modeling • Listening • Communication

Remember: Inviting children to speak the truth requires your being able to hear the truth.

One day, Scott said in a stern tone of voice, "You have a problem today and I'm not it." He was correct. His right to express those feelings without creating a major drama allowed an otherwise volatile situation to immediately dissipate.

What is the difference between lack of respect and telling the truth? I think tone of voice, body language and choice of words are the key issues. There is a vast difference between the following ways to say something:

NO: "You are always picking one me. I never do anything right. All you do is nag, nag, nag! You never say anything nice to me. "(Yelling, screaming, pouting, and stomping.)

YES: "I don't feel as if I can do anything right today. I hate it when you're mad at me. I'm having a hard day too, OK? " (Friendly body language, words, tone of voice.)

Are you willing to hear the truth? Do you realize that since there was no school on how to parent this child, you might be making a few mistakes? And can your child point out a mistake without causing a war? How you talk to your children will teach them how to talk to you and others:

No: "What's this report card about, young man?"
Yes: "How do you feel about this card? (Response). What is one thing you could do differently to change the (Math) grade? How about a tutor?"

No: "I don't care if you're angry, you don't yell and scream in this house. "(yelling)
Yes: "If you are that angry, why don't you run down the street and back. We can talk when you cool down a little."

No: "There's nothing to cry about. (Blah! Blah! Blah!)"
Yes: "Go ahead, cry. We'll talk about it when you can."

No: "Who do you think you are talking to in that tone of voice?"
Yes: "I really want to hear what you're saying, and my ears just can't listen to that tone of voice. Start over please, with a tone of voice I can hear."

TELLING THE TRUTH

> Essential Ingredients
> Modeling • Patience • Perspective

Remember: We do not live in a world where the truth is honored or valued. Telling the truth is not an easy skill.

Telling the truth does not mean you "let it all hang out" with your children. Some things are none of their business. When your child asks you if there is something wrong and there is, change the usual response of "Nothing," to, "I'm upset about something that doesn't concern you. Thanks for caring about me, and I need some space to work it out by myself.

When your children turn into teenagers, it is part of their home-work for breaking away and becoming independent to not share every-thing with you. If you model the truth when they are young, you will hear, "Sorry Mom, I don't want to talk about it. I'm ok", rather than some trumped up story to shut you up.

Rather than treating lying from a small child as a huge atrocity, remember that every action has a cause. Maybe the pressure you are cre-ating is cause for the lie. The way you phrase a question and your tone of voice has a lot to do with what response you might get: "Did you eat the cookies, young man?" infers that death is eminent and any wise child will head straight for denial. Instead say something like, "I see several cookies have been eaten and since the cookie monster isn't visiting us today, I bet it was you!" (Child admits the truth.) "Well, I want you to ask me before you eat a treat next time. Do you understand?"

The issue above is the eaten cookies. When pressured into lying one issue turns into two, cookies *and* lying. If you turn every single issue into two issues, it gets to be a very long day. Watch **how** you phrase each question.

When a child does not tell the truth, treat everything said there-after with a question mark. An annoyed child will ask, "Don't you trust/believe me?" You might respond, "I believed you until you chose to give me reason not to — now I am not sure whether you are choosing to tell the truth or not." Tired of being monitored, the child will ask for another chance to be trusted with the truth.

GIVING YOUR WORD

> Essential Ingredients:
> Modeling • Patience • Communication

Remember: You teach most by modeling.

Since my children were little, there has been built a sacred trust that none of us will break. When we give our word it will not be broken.

"I give you my word" are words they heard when they were small. Never, under any circumstances did I break my word. Therefore, when I say those words, there is no question as to their authenticity.

I travel around the country giving workshops to adults. When I am on the road, sometimes I'm asked, "How do you know your teenagers aren't using your house for a party while you are gone?" The answer is unfathomable to most who ask that question: "They gave me their word they wouldn't."

When you are teaching a child to keep his/her word, it is important not to treat any breaking of their word as an atrocity. The problem is simple, "I want to trust your word is good. When you keep your word I can do that; when you break your word I don't know when to trust you or when not to trust you. You can't keep your word sometimes. You must keep it at all times, even if it is hard to do. Next time you give your word, you need to keep it."

Similar to the process used in teaching children to tell the truth, when a child breaks his/her word, the next time something comes up in which their word is given openly distrust that they will follow through and keep it. When the child is upset because there is a lack of trust, talk about it in this way, "I want us to trust each other. The last time you gave your word there was a problem keeping it. I'm not sure when you mean it and when you don't." When your child asks for another chance, give it. Repeat the process with less willingness to give another chance if the infraction continues. Some children have a built-in code of ethics which, for some reason, they would not violate — the others simply need some coaching.

I think you teach integrity by having integrity. There are a lot of things I simply wouldn't do because it is out of integrity with whom I have chosen to be — both children understand and emulate those characteristics.

TEACHING MANNERS

> Essential Ingredients:
> Modeling • Patience • Humor

Remember: What is easy for you may not be easy for your child—coach with kindness.

You are in the market with your dressed-beautifully, darling child. A friend comes up and you want your child to have good manners.

Most of us are terrified of meeting new people; children are not the exception. If you meet up with a friend and your chatty child becomes deaf, dumb and looks down, it is best not to call your child "shy" or make excuses for the behavior. Let it go.

When the friend leaves, get down on your child's level and ask, "Mrs. Bauer has the most beautiful eyes. Do you know what color they are? " Your child, never having looked at the person will not know, so you respond, "Next time someone talks to us, you take a peek and after they leave tell me the color of that person's eyes...OK?"

Looking into the eyes of a person is the beginning of teaching a child to relate to other people. Manners follow easily with self-trust.

I don't force my children to shake hands and say "How do you do?" After one of my children has met someone I might say, "Sometimes, when I meet someone for the first time, I feel uncomfortable. I shake hands with people because it gives me something to do other than to stand there and feel foolish. Sometimes, I ask a question so they will talk until I feel better. 'How are you?' or 'Do you like the rain we are having?' are questions that give breathing space."

It is helpful if you give your child something to say. "Scott, this is Mrs. Hoffner. She is Doug's mother and she said you and Doug drew a wonderful picture at school today." The child, having been reminded of something he knows about and got praised for, will probably chatter away in response.

Practice these skills at home by role playing. Simply set up a situation (What if we were at the drug store and my friend, John, the coach came up to us. What could I say that would help you to feel more comfortable?) Then act it out. Practicing with you is safe and gives the child the resource to "do it for real" under the pressure of every-day life.

TEACHING MANNERS #2

Essential Ingredients:
Modeling • Patience • Awareness

Remember: Teach your standards for manners with respect for the child who wants to please you.

In today's world the standard for manners is almost non-existent. A man isn't sure whether opening the door for a woman will be appreciated or renounced as an insult.

As stated earlier, I think manners stem from true respect more than acting respectful. If my son opened (or even tried to open the door for me) I'd nod and said, "I appreciate your manners, thank you!"

The dinner table can become a combat zone where tempers fly instead of creating an atmosphere of togetherness and sharing. Correcting a child in front of everyone else always causes a problem. A quiet signal to one child about the napkin belonging in the lap, chewing with your mouth shut, sitting up straight, getting your elbow off the table or some other misdemeanor saves face and is a true teacher.

Remember my father's rule of leadership: Corrections are to be given behind the barn (in private), accolades shouted from the rooftops.

I stand up when someone older comes into the room (now that my hair is grey, I seldom perform this act any more!) My children asked me why I do that. My answer is simple: "It is the way I was raised. We discard older people in our society. Just by living as long as they have an older person has more experience in life than I do — I stand up in respect to that difference." Both children heard that statement and for a long time, did nothing with the information. Recently, I noticed, they stand when someone older approaches them. Their standing, as a matter of true respect, is received as such by the beholder.

There is a vast difference between respecting people and pretending to have good manners — one is useless without the other.

TEACHING MANNERS #3

> Essential Ingredients:
> Modeling • Patience • Communication

Remember: Manners reflect respect.

Some parents are so hung up on manners that their little chicks become veritable robots, chanting meaningless phrases as a means of escaping their parent's wrath rather than caring a hoot about being respectful.

I am seldom amused when a parent says to the child, in front of me, "Say thank you." The "thank you" which is returned has no feeling or meaning in it.

Do I think manners are important? Yes. I teach them by modeling. I treat my children with respect and verbally appreciate them whenever possible. I never ask them to do something without saying "please" and use my best manners on them. My friends are inherited and will come and go — my children are forever a part of me.

If my child receives something from another person and says nothing, I give a signal or suggest the "thank you" without being noticed by giver. Would you tell your wife or husband, "Say thank you, (name)" when someone pours them a glass of wine? Ridiculous! Respect begets respect. Treat your child with respect at all times.

Talk to your children about ways they could have handled a situation differently. Role play with them so they can practice what may not be easy for them to do in public: "Let's act out the part where we went to dinner with grandma and grandpa. I'll pretend I am you and you help me with what I could say." Working on solutions together is a wonderful means of being close to your child, and gives that child a tool for his/her life.

Recently, Scott was watching a basketball game. I told him some friends were coming over and I'd like him to come into the living room and chat for a few minutes. He protested. I said simply, "Scott, it is important to me that you do this. I'm sorry about interrupting your game. Whether you want to tape what you miss or not, I want you to come in and pleasantly chat with my friends for a little while." He was not thrilled with my plan — but he did what I asked. Had Scott joined us and been grumpy I would have excused both of us and said to him, "Being grumpy to get even with me won't work. You need to be pleasant and charming or there will be a consequence. Do we need to discuss the consequence, or are you ready to be charming?" There was no need for such talk on this occasion because Scott already knows I won't allow such behavior.

RESPECT PRIVACY

> Essential Ingredients:
> Trust • Respect • Honoring Rights

Remember: Each and every person has a right to privacy.

During the course of your child's life, the need for privacy will change many times, but the right of that child to have privacy will not.

Many parents choose to search a child's room for notes and other information. Unless there is cause for such action (suspicion of drug use for one), I think such an intrusion builds distrust, resentment and builds a wall between the parent and child.

One morning, I was putting something on Kathleen's bed and her phone rang. While talking, I noticed a school paper on the floor. It was a story. I love the way Kathleen writes, so after the call, read the story. That night, I said something about liking her story and her response was, "Why were you reading things in my room?" I explained what had happened and apologized for the intrusion into her privacy.

The next day I noticed Kathleen had left some notes by the computer, and there was another story. This time it was in my room — and it was still her story. So I put the papers on her bed with a note saying, "You left this by the computer. I am curious to read your story, and I didn't without your permission (Mother-in-training: Looks like there is hope!). Next morning, the story was on my desk with a note, "Mom: Thanks for asking...hope you like this story."

Never, under any circumstances do I read either child's mail — or grade cards which are addressed to them. In working with teens across the country, I see a lot of resentment towards parents for reading mail which is not theirs. The point made is that it is none of the parent's business. And, unless, as I said before, there is a reason other than general distrust, their point is valid.

When you check up on a child every minute and question each action, the message given seems clear: I do not trust you to do your own life. There is a difference between being a warden and a coach. A warden has to stay in prison to keep charge of the prisoner — so both sides build resentment.

At night, I like to know where my teens are going and with whom. In the daytime, I really don't care.

A coach guides, suggests, offers assistance, asks for information, sets limits, gives consequences and respects the right for privacy.

TEACHING HOW TO SAVE MONEY

> Essential Ingredients:
> Communication • Standards • Don't Give In

Remember: Learning to save money is an essential skill for survival in the adult world.

Since there are classes and courses for adults in how to spend money wisely, we may assume this skill is not an inherited one. With the advent of plastic credit cards came a new problem: indebtedness. People I know have even lost their homes because they did not carefully monitor their spending.

Your child really wants a toy or something in particular. It costs eight dollars with tax (be sure to teach that tax makes the price higher). Your child gets one dollar a week for allowance.

Writing on a piece of paper, put the amount needed. Write down how much money comes in each week. Figure out how long it will take to buy the item if nothing else is added besides the allowance. Eight weeks is too long? OK, let's look at the extra chore list and see what you could do to quickly earn the money needed.

Sometimes it is fun and appropriate to do matching funds: "For every dollar you earn I will put in a dollar." Such action allows you to contribute to the item and still maintain the integrity of child in being responsible.

A piggy bank or savings account are wonderful ways for the child to do some long-term saving. Matching funds can be an incentive here to: "For every dollar you put into your account, I will put in fifty cents." Be careful, however, to consider the outcome of having a child who is a prodigious saver — you could owe a lot of money!

Again, your job is to teach your child that things have value and that there is often more involved in having something than just getting it. Children who are taught to respect spending are less likely to put themselves through the horror of a large indebtedness as an adult.

OPENLY CARE ABOUT PEOPLE AND THE WORLD

> Essential Ingredients:
> Modeling • Self-trust • Let Yourself Care

Remember: Most of what your children learn is what you model.

Many people hide their caring because they are afraid of rejection. I don't like rejection any more than anyone else, and have learned that what is perceived by me as rejection is often someone else's fear (usually of being rejected!).

When I was a child, I would sit and talk to my grandmother while she baked. If she heard a siren she would stop, raise her forefinger into the air and close her eyes for a second. When I asked what she was doing, she explained, "Someone is in trouble. I raise my finger as an affirmation to my thought: God got there first! " That was over forty years ago. To this day, whenever I hear a siren, I raise my forefinger and.....

One day, I was watching Scott playing basketball. A siren could be heard. In a split second, I saw his forefinger raised into the air.....

We got the call that Scott had fallen out of a tree and was badly hurt. Driving away from the house Kathleen asked, "Mom, is Scott going to be OK?" I answered as calmly as I could, "I don't know, but what we do know is God got there first!"

The other night, Kathleen asked if I knew some family. I didn't. It seems their house had been robbed, and she just thought I might send them some love. (Sometimes, the forefinger isn't necessary.)

I go for a walk every morning. They are remodeling the house across the street, so I stop in on my way in to check out the crew's progress. Whenever I drive out of my driveway, the crew members wave to me. The other day, my car battery was dead. The guys across the street had the battery jumped and running in no time. Am I friendly so I will get something? No. I get something by being friendly.

I get really upset when people kill animals or hurt the earth. I openly cry at whales being killed, an oil slick killing animals or some other atrocity of man to nature. I am equally emotional about people hurting each other. My openness is a statement of caring that both of my children emulate.

TEACHING RESPECT FOR THE EARTH

> Essential Ingredients:
> Modeling • Awareness • Communication

Remember: We must care about each other and about the well-being of our earth in order to survive the mistakes of the past.

Recently, my teenagers and I were recounting past memories. One of the heartiest sessions came when they told how I would drag them clear across town just to see a tree, or would stop the car and have everyone look at the sunset. Appreciation is best taught by appreciating.

In this fast-paced, high technological world it is easy to get very mental. It is essential we teach our children to create a balance between their mind and their heart. Without compassion we cannot protect the very world on which we are dependent — and we will not love each other enough to live here peacefully. Compassion comes with understanding.

Talk to your children. Show them the results of a forest fire, the effects of erosion, creatures killed by oil, and go for a walk with them in an area that has not been harmed.

Watch nature programs to discover the wonder of the earth on which we all live.

Talk about what the world will look like if each of us throws paper out the car window or carelessly to the ground. Something each of us can do is to stop littering the world with our trash. Something your family can do together is to go to a nearby lot or park with trash bags and pick up an area together.

We feel helpless because our problems are so big, but if each of us stops being complacent and does something, destroying our earth will stop.

Get involved in saving the Rain Forest in Brazil — if it is destroyed, we will not be able to breathe. This is not an issue for someone else, it is an issue for each one of us.

When was the last time you walked out in nature and thought about the wonder of whatever you saw? We have been given this earth and we are destroying it. It is a bad dream from which each of us must awaken — and be certain the dream does not become a reality.

If you want your children to care about the earth, you must care about it and invite them to join you.

ENCOURAGE YOUR CHILDREN TO BE FRIENDS

Essential Ingredients:
Awareness • Empathy • Communication

Remember: If your children are friends, each one will always have an ally in life.

One of my greatest joys is that my two children are very close friends. They care about and support each other. It is helpful that one is a boy and the other a girl, so there is no competition in terms of sex — and I think there are things one can do to assist in building a friendship:

1. Never compare one child to the other. Each child is unique and special, and nothing like the other(s). If one child does well in school and the other does not, it probably has nothing to do with intelligence. One is a student, one is not, which has nothing to do with individual value.

2. Don't make one child the mother. Assisting with a small child is a requirement of being the eldest child, and it is important that too much responsibility is not given (which may build resentment).

3. Separate the person from his/her behavior so you are always giving the message that it is behavior not the person with which you are upset. Instead of, "You lazy bum.." (insulting the person) say, "I don't like it when dishes are left everywhere, and..." (Focus on the behavior.)

4. Make it a non-optional rule to only use "I" messages when fighting. Be sure you uphold this rule as well. (See page 76)

5. Teach your children how to communicate their feelings so things do not go underground and fester.

6. Ask one child to assist the other when it is appropriate — and express your appreciation for that assistance.

Children who are friends have more fun, create more harmony in the home and create a supportive foundation for the numerous struggles in life.

FRIENDSHIP

> Essential Ingredients:
> Communication • Patience • Trust

Remember: Your child is learning about him/herself through friendships.

At the end of sixth grade, Kathleen and I were talking. Suddenly, she exploded in self-recrimination. "I can't believe I was so dumb! I did everything I could to get into the sociable group (most popular girls). Well, I got in, and guess what? Nothing in common is what! I can't believe I wasted a whole year of my life with that nonsense!" I laughed because I love how honest Kathleen is with herself, and said through mounting pride, "Well, if you learn at eleven that being in a group you don't want to be in means compromise or death, you've not wasted a year. I love you!"

When Scott was about nine, we were vacationing at Catalina Island. Each of my children had taken a friend with whom to play. One morning, Scott and Matt had already been fishing, bike riding and Scott was currently throwing himself off the Avalon float into the water,only to get up and throw himself off again. Matt was sitting on a towel on the beach. As I walked up next to him, Matt's eyes stayed on Scott as he spoke, "Maybe if we don't feed him lunch, he will run out of gas." When children pick a friend to go on vacation, be sure to encourage choosing one with similar interests — it is a long week (or two) if there is a mismatch!

Driving to soccer one day, I asked Kathleen and Betsy to describe their favorite meal. Betsy began,"Loster..Bisque.. no just plain lobster with lots of butter..and fruit compote..peach melba...and if mother would let me, of course, wine." In her droll, marvelous way, Kathleen said, "Hope it isn't my turn 'cause all I can think of is a grilled cheese sandwich." Neither girl understood why I laughed all the way to their practice.

The ability to have friends and still maintain your own sense of identity is an art that few children or adults have mastered. There is nothing more difficult than trying to teach your child to never compromise on his/her own integrity and to quietly remain true to him/herself. How do you do that? You guessed it, modeling — plus setting appropriate standards and communicating lots of idea and feelings so the child can choose appropriately for him/herself.

CHOOSING FRIENDS

> Essential Ingredients:
> Communication • Trust • Patience

Remember: It is your child's homework to break away from you and develop friendships.

There are few things that are more difficult than to watch your child engage in a friendship that you know is going to turn out badly. (Wait until the teen years when dating is the game!) It is seldom works to prohibit a child from being with another child because they can meet anyway.

I remember once, Scott had a playmate I didn't trust. So I told Scott my truth: "I have an uncomfortable feeling when Jacob is around. Because I don't trust him, I would rather you choose a different person to play with. I also don't mess with your friendships. So I want you to play with Jacob outside of our home. I can help you with the words to say to him, and I don't want you to bring Jacob in our home. Do you have anything you want to say about this?" Scott didn't. We followed my rule. The relationship soon ended.

Fortunately, neither of my children have had boy or girl friends I really didn't like — or who looked like the local drug users or pushers. As I look back on my many friendships, not all of my choices were wise ones, so it seems unreasonable for me not to expect my children to experiment in their choices.

One day, a neighbor came up to me in the market and dressed me down because Kathleen did not invite her daughter to her birthday party. Recovering from my surprise, I said, "I do not choose Kathleen's friends for her. If Gwen is upset with Kathleen she needs to talk to Kathleen about it. I am not going to fight with you over something that is none of my business."

This same parent called me saying it was a shame that her daughter and mine didn't play together as they were the same age. Stating the obvious, I remarked, "Maybe they don't want to be friends," to which the mother replied, "Well, Gwen wants to be friends with Kathleen, but..." Cutting her off, I stated, "I think it is up to the two girls to decide whether they are going to be friends or not. I do not interfere in my children's relationships."

As some point, Gwen and Kathleen became friends. The mother phoned one afternoon asking where the girls were. I said they had taken my car and gone to lunch. When I didn't know exactly where they had gone (which I didn't care to know) the mother said Gwen could no longer be with Kathleen. It is best to stay out of our children's friendships.

HAVING FRIENDS OVER

> Essential Ingredients:
> Generosity • Patience • Communication

Remember: If your child chooses friends wisely, that support system may be the difference in social and personal choices.

For some reason the percentage of my kids having someone over compared to them going elsewhere was about ten to one. My mother didn't like to have company, especially the spur of the moment kind — so I tend to be in the "we can manage one more" category.

The craving for "sleep-overs" begins at an earlier age than I remember for me. For the parents the benefits are that, sometimes, both children will stay at someone else's house on the same night (this is about as rare, however as both tots taking a nap at the same time when they were little). The other side of the coin is that instead of two children you have three or four for two days and a night. In the rule book that all children read before being born, it says, "Never, ever sleep at a sleep-over." Giggling is what girls do, building forts in the night is what boys do. My rule was simple: Stay in your bedroom and don't leave the house (once they went out the window, so that rule became necessary). Socialization is a fundamental part of your child's development — sleep-overs are part of the process.

If you don't like surprises (5:30 at night when you have just enough dinner for your own family, "Mom, can Doug spend the night?") have a rule to include requiring two hours' notice. Maybe you begin the sleep-over after dinner.

When my children ask anything in front of a friend, the answer is automatically, "No!" with no refunds.

Scott's best friend, Doug mostly lives with us on week- ends and all summer. I try to treat Doug the same as I do Scott. When they come out in the morning, I give both of them a hug. When they leave a mess, I get upset with both of them. When I need help with something, I ask both of them.

From time-to-time, Doug's mother says she should pay me monthly food and recreational costs. I figure best friends are a good investment — for both of them. Neither Scott or Doug are doin' drugs or anything that bothers me (other than leaving their sweatsocks in my car). Having Doug as Scott's support person is worth ten times the cost of his presence. Besides, I love Doug, too.

WHAT YOUR CHILDREN'S FRIENDS CONTRIBUTE TO YOUR LIFE

Essential Ingredients:
Sense of Humor • Trust • Communication

Remember: Though it is not your place to remain a play-mate to your children, some great memories are found in tom-foolery.

Scott and Doug Hoffner have been best friends for many years. They are the world's leading champions at harmless horse-play. At times, I've been a part of their craziness:

My friend, Darlene and I were walking out of the show one night, following Scott and Doug. An occasional M&M candy would hit us. Neither boy looked around, there was just a sudden rain of little candies. Finally, I looked at Darlene saying, "I've had enough, how about you?"

Taking another bag of candy from my purse, we took handfulls of candy and started after them. Boys have a certain instinct about pending ambushes, so both Doug and Scott took off on a dead run.

I had my hand cocked, ready to launch some candies at one of my targets when a police car screeched to a halt right behind me, and a policeman jumped out, gun-in-hand. I could see the headlines, "Self-Esteem Activist Arrested for M&M Fight!" There was a robbery in the next shopping center and the police thought we were running away from it.

One Saturday the doorbell rang. No one was there. I went back inside and the doorbell rang again. I walked out almost to the end of the entry way, and something caught my eye; it was the shadow of my son, standing on the roof, waiting to pour a bucket of water on his dear mother. Quietly, I moved sideways, turned on the garden hose and sprang forth, getting him broad-side. It was a victorious moment for this middle-aged woman.

Most of the time, Scott and Doug get busy sailing water balloons off the cliff, having shaving cream fights, playing ping-pong with cracked Christmas tree ornaments, cutting up Boogie Boards to make "hand guns" for body surfing, or some other creative play. It is fun to once-in-awhile be a part of their foolishness. I think it is also vital that the offer to play is invitational, not mandatory. When I don't want to be in the game I say so, and that request is honored. No teenager needs a 48 year old buddy; I am a parent first, a playmate next. And...once in awhile, it does my heart good to join into their fun.

COMMUNICATION SKILLS AND FEELINGS

USING "I" INSTEAD OF "YOU" MESSAGES

> Essential Ingredients:
> Awareness • Communication • Perseverance

Remember: Using "I" messages honors the BEING and focuses on changing behavior.

My daughter just turned nineteen. There is gray in my hair. And I have a treasure chest of memories to carry me through the time when she leaves — for we have loved each other every single day since she was born. We have not always gotten along, and we have honored our differences by using "I" messages.

"Y-O-U" messages are about a child's being: "You are a bum, a pig, a pain in the ....." are messages which are arrows to the heart of a child. Some of those arrows are never removed throughout that individual's life. **Listen to what you are saying to your child.**

Start with the word "I" and focus on your child's behavior:

"I have a problem with the backpack by the front door."

"I am concerned that your homework isn't being done."

"I would like to hear what you are saying, but my ears can't listen to that tone-of-voice. Would you change your tone-of-voice so I can listen to you?"

"I want you to go into the other room. When I get off the phone I will come and see you."

Using a formula from the book PROJECT SELF-ESTEEM, express your feelings and then say your wants.

"I'm upset with the mess in the livingroom, and I want you to go pick it up right now."

"It is upsetting when you don't keep your promises. I want to trust you and I can do that when you keep your word."

Saying, "I don't like what you did," is a far different message than I don't like you because you did something. Children who are raised with conditional love learn to disregard the feelings of others. Often they choose people who withhold giving love to their mates.

PRACTICE: USING "I" INSTEAD OF "YOU" MESSAGES

Suggestion: Read each problem and discuss with your mate what you might say in that situation. Be sure to use an "I" message—and remember that these examples are MY way — not the right way.

1. YOUR CHILD STARTS TALKING WHILE YOU ARE TALKING.

No: "You're rude! Don't you know it's wrong to....."

Yes: "I'm sure what you have to say is important and I want you to wait until I finish talking."

2. YOUR CHILD FORGOT TO TAKE OUT THE TRASH.

No: "What's the matter with you? Do I have to do everything around here?"

Yes: "I was really angry when I noticed you forgot to take out the trash. I want you to take it out right now. If you forget to take it out next time, you will be volunteering to get the trash in all the rooms in our house."

3. YOUR CHILD IS WATCHING A LOT OF TELEVISION.

No: "You watch too much TV. You are lazy. Don't you know too much television is bad for you?"

Yes: "I want you to watch less television. Starting tomorrow there will be no television until your chores are done. Also, there will be no TV in this house for anyone from 6:00 to 8:00 p.m. each school night. There will be no television in the mornings before school, either. We'll try it for a week and see how it works."

4. YOUR CHILD SPILLS FOOD ON HIS/HER NEW PANTS.

No: "You're a bad (girl/boy) for spilling your food!"

Yes: "Looks like your pants need a wash. Come with me and I'll teach you how to do a load of wash."

Note: Starting at age nine, both of my children do their own wash. They need to set a day for doing their wash, check with each other to be sure the washer will be free, and remember to do it. A timer will assist in remembering to move the wash to the dryer. Lessons on washing light colors separate from dark colors is a must. Also talk about proper use of the dryer.

HIDDEN MESSAGES BUILD DISTRUST

> Essential Ingredients:
> Communicate • Truth • Listen

Remember: The truth is not automatically spoken unless it is given on both sides.

This morning, I fixed a wonderful breakfast for my sixteen year old son, Scott. He spoke no words of exclamation or joy. Then I heard myself say, to his statement about sour juice, "Well not everybody's mother gets up and fixes breakfast in the morning!" Scott frowned at my sudden outburst.

The sour juice has nothing to do with wanting a compliment about my great breakfast. Instead I could have said, "I'd like a compliment about the breakfast you are eating, please!"

If you model asking for compliments, your children are less likely to devise endless manipulative games in order to get compliments. Anyone's fear in asking for compliments is rejection. Sometimes, when I ask my children for a compliment, I get a crazy response. (To my request for a breakfast compliment): "This isn't a bad breakfast if you like dinosaur eggs and homemade hashbrowns". Laugh at the attempt towards humor and hang in there with, "I like your joke and am still waiting for my compliment, please."

Express what you are feeling and ask for what you want. Frequently expressing your feelings and wants makes it less likely that little irritations will accumulate and turn into a major explosions. People who save up their anger tend to go on tirades. Irrational anger teaches the child to fear the individual. It does **not** encourage new behavior for the child.

Each child is a unique, wondrous treasure chest of perceptions and feelings. To give one child the hidden message that you prefer the other child devalues the many gifts each child can bring to you. Usually, the child you have the most difficulty getting along with is the one most like you. In devaluing him/her you are doing the same to yourself. Love your children separately. Never compare, especially verbally.

ASKING FOR A REPLAY

> Essential Ingredients:
> Humility • Asking for a Replay • Sense of Humor

Remember: You don't need to stay entrenched in something when it is going badly.

Recently, I stopped Scott to talk to him about something. I wasn't irritated with him or wanting to reprimand him for anything, and yet the conversation slowly started to slide towards a war zone. Becoming aware that we were "losing it", I said, "Stop! (Time out sign with my hands). Let's do a replay, this is going downhill fast." I started with my original comment and we literally re-did the conversation, by-passing the place where we somehow bumped off of each other.

This morning (just to prove I can write this stuff and am learning to use it all the time) I turned to Scott who was using the phone in my den, and said, "Do you hear the trash truck? You'd better hope its going up the other side cuz I'm going to have your head if our trash doesn't get out this week!" He raised his eyebrows and said quite calmly, "I put the trash out first thing this morning." I looked at him remorsefully saying, "Gosh, wonder where that talk came from. May I have a replay?" He smiled and responded, "No need, it's OK." And we both let it go.

Old patterns are difficult to break. Children and adults who are learning new ways of communicating need a place to practice, do it incorrectly, and try again.

It's difficult to undo what is done. You **can** acknowledge that you **want** to communicate differently and that you **are** willing to learn a new way. Being flexible is the key to learning to communicate in a way that is honest and fully expresses feelings. Forgiveness is unnecessary when everyone in the family acknowledges that learning to work together is a process. Mistakes are a natural part of people learning to live and work together.

A replay requires that no one blames anyone for what is going wrong. The action is stopped and each participant agrees to go back through the conversation, taking responsibility for changing words that caused friction. Who started the problem is irrelevant. Two people are working together to stop the problem from escalating. The rules are very basic: Be truthful, non-judging, flexible, listen, and take responsibility for your part, only.

WAR WORDS ARE UNNECESSARY

> Essential Ingredients:
> Self-discipline • Listen to Yourself • Patience

Remember: One hastily-chosen set of words can scar your child for life.

There are words that bring up an automatic "fight" response from others. Avoiding such words assists in keeping on purpose rather than creating a fight over something totally unrelated to the subject at hand.

Words to avoid are: SHOULD, OUGHT, MUST, HAVE TO and EVERYBODY. To check out your own response to these words, pair off with your husband or a friend and say the following sentences to them, using a stern tone of voice.

1. You should keep the house clean.
2. You really ought to learn to get to places on time.
3. You must take the trash out today.
4. You have to be polite even if you don't feel like it.
5. Everybody likes parties, you should, too.

Chances are, your rebellious little kid had some resistance to those words. My point is not to outlaw these words, but to use them judiciously and only when well-chosen. "You should drive on the right side of the road," is the truth.

Let's do those same sentences and replace the "prison" words with "freedom" words: WANT, WISH, CHOOSE, DESIRE and PREFER.

1. I (want) you to keep the house clean.
2. Please (choose) to get to places on time.
3. I (want) you to take the trash out today, please.
4. I (want) you to be polite even if you don't feel like it.
5. If you don't (wish) to go to the party, that's OK.

Having taught my children to be quite literal in their speech, I didn't foresee the problems that could occur: My sister arrived for a family outing, asked Scott if he wanted to help her, he checked inside himself and said, "No thanks." I overheard the conversation, leaned out of the door and said to my skateboarding son, "Scott, I can see you are having fun and Aunt Shelley needs a hand right now, please." He hopped off his board and happily assisted. In our home, the question, "Do you want.." is not a command, but a question.

AVOIDING "GOOD" AND "BAD" AS WORDS

> Essential Ingredients:
> Listen to Yourself • Patience • Understanding

Remember: Every "good" and "bad" message given to a child is translated into "good person" or "bad person."

When I taught elementary school, I noticed that most children were brought up to value everything they did in terms of good and bad. What surprised me was that these good and bad messages were recorded in the child's own valuing system as messages about their BEING.

As a teacher, it is easy to respond to a child's answer with the word "good". What is the opposite of good? (bad). Such labeling puts the whole class in jeopardy. It switched a simple matter of discovering an answer into a matter of being good or bad which they translated into being a good or a bad person.

When a little girl ties her shoe, saying "You're such a good girl!" is not a positive statement. "I like how you tied your shoe!" is the TRUTH, PERSONAL and SPECIFIC.

When a little boy actually picks up a dish and takes it into the kitchen (even when learned, they forget this behavior in their teens), "Good boy!" needs to be replaced with, "Thanks for taking your dish out, Scott." Such a comment is PERSONAL and SPECIFIC.

When a child tries to set the table (whether it is done properly or not), avoid "Good girl or boy!" Say instead, "I noticed you set the table. Thank you."

When a child is naughty, it is the behavior that needs correcting, not the BEING of the child. "You are a bad boy!" doesn't tell the child anything about the problem. Instead, "I don't want you to hit your sister. You are to use your words!" states the **PROBLEM and YOUR DESIRE.**

It isn't easy to personalize each message, and it is personalized messages that teach and nurture your children.

CHORES AND ALLOWANCE

> Essential Ingredients:
> Teach How • Communication • Consequences

Remember: To feel a part of a group, there needs to be some sort of responsibility to that group.

Let me begin by saying I do not put chores and allowance together. I give a weekly living allowance to each child (which is always the same amount and is dependent upon individual needs). Recreational activities and the food each child chooses to eat out of the home are paid for with their allowance. As you know, giving five dollars here and five dollars there (even for such a good cause as the fun and pleasure of your child) can add up to a lot of money.

Things like shampoo, hair spray, tampax, and toothpaste are not in their cost of living expenses as children. I keep a jug with twenty dollars in it for those things. No questions are asked about that money, and I check it periodically to see if it needs replenishing. How do I know my children don't take that money for other things? Because I don't ask them to tell me what they use it for and yet they always do: "Mom I bought some toothpaste today and took money from the jug." Beyond that, it is a matter of trust and honor — those things are taught from birth.

Chores are a part of being responsible to the well-being of the home. In our home there are chores which are expected to be done and a list of chores that can be done to earn some extra money. I have found that giving teenagers a reasonable time limit in which to accomplish their chore works better than the "do it now" version: "Kathleen, the dishwasher needs to be emptied. Please do so before dinner tonight."

I am against "boy chores" and "girl chores". Make a list of all the things that need to be done in order to have the home functioning properly. Be sure to put "going to work" on the list and "taking care of the children" as both are jobs. As a family, discuss the list and have individuals volunteer for specific jobs. Some jobs (like cleaning out the garage) may be a family job which needs to be scheduled on a week- end. The point is to involve the child in deciding which jobs he/she can do, and to let that child be aware of the over-all scope of jobs necessary to maintain a home.

WHAT IS A REASONABLE CHORE?

> Essential Ingredients:
> Patience • Communication • Kindness

Remember: Asking a child to do something he/she is unable to do negatively effects his/her self-esteem.

Many of the parenting and child development books have guidelines for ages and which chores are appropriate. I generally followed my instinct in this matter.

Small children like to be busy and love to please. To ask a small child to empty to silverware section of the dishwasher is possible. Be aware that your drawer may cease to have neat rows of forks, knives, etc. after this job is accomplished—and feeling useful is so much more important than neat piles. Be careful to remove any sharp knives or other harmful items.

A small child can separate laundry by finding one item: "See if you can find all of Daddy's T-shirts that look like this!"

A small child may be given a rag with some oil to dust or with cleaning solution to clean. If you need to oil or clean over the spot he/she did, *remember to do it privately, later.*

Young children can set the table, fold laundry, help take out the trash, make their own bed, pick up a mess, vacuum a small area, dust, dry silverware, water flowers, help wash the car, and other "little hands" activities.

Teenagers are obviously capable of doing anything an adult can do. Finding time in their busy schedule for chores seems to be their biggest issue. In learning time management, a teen needs to schedule accomplishing chores into his/her schedule. I give my two teens a list of things that need to be done and a reasonable time in which to do it. A consequence for not meeting my deadline is to do the chore(s) on "their time" (television, play time, etc.).

When one of them trails off, constantly forgetting to get chores done, we sit down and have a talk about how to get back on track. We make an agreement, and if that agreement is not kept, I give specific orders on specific days (and even stand watch over the teen until it is accomplished). Eventually, the teen will ask for the right to choose for him/herself again. The keys to success are PERSISTENCE and CONSISTENCY.

Chores are done for the right to live in your home and to be a part of your family.

WHEN CHORES DON'T GET DONE, WHAT DO YOU DO?

> Essential Ingredients:
> Patience • Communication • Humor

Remember: You are the coach, training your child to be responsible.

One of the ways children can drive parents to the border of insanity is by failing to do chores. Sometimes this act is one of rebellion, sometimes it has to do with the way the individual child's mind functions and sometimes it has to do with the day itself. The quest is to have your child take care of his/her chore without making you the warden.

1. Be sure there is clarity as to what is expected, both in **what** the job is and in **how** it is to be done.

2. Set reasonable time limits for the job to be accomplished: "You will have your floor cleaned off and everything on it put away before you leave this morning, OK?"

3. Assist the child in remembering that the chore exists: "I am putting a string over your two fingers, please do not remove it until the trash is out in front of the house." (Some children remember, some need reminders; I have a dear friend who changes the ring on her finger to remind her to do or get something. She has taught herself to honor her need for a physical reminder and not set herself up for endless apologies or excuses.)

4. Help a child remember what day it is: "It's Wednesday, trash goes out today, please!" Some children know what day it is and what happens in that day— other children need more training to overview each day.

5. Be firm in making an agreement and expecting that the agreement is kept:

    A: "We had an agreement about the mess in the living room."
    B: "Oh, yeah! I forgot, sorry!"
    A: "The living room needs your attention right now."
    B: "I will, I promise I will when I get back!"
    A: "Sorry. Our agreement was that it would be picked up before lunch. It is after lunch. It needs to be done, now."
    B: "Mom, I'll be late!"
    A: "Now, please."

If a child fails to keep an agreement in doing a chore, have it done on "their time." They get the point...eventually!

LISTEN TO YOUR CHILD'S NEEDS AND HONOR THEM

> Essential Ingredients:
> Listening • Hearing • Communication

Remember: Often, communication is non-verbal. Watch your children for clues to their real feelings.

When Scott was seven, he became enormously despondent because his older sister, Kathleen had won several trophies and he had never won even one. My job as a parent was to honor his feelings, not downplay his sister's achievement to protect him. Of course, I wanted to do something that assisted him with his feelings.

Saying, "Don't worry, you will get a trophy some day," didn't lessen his pain. He wanted a trophy today. So we began to talk about reasonable things he could do in his own life to earn a trophy. He decided to work really hard in soccer. Unfortunately, his soccer team did not win a trophy that season. Not only that, none of his sports activities brought him a trophy that year.

Kathleen's room began to fill with trophies from sports and other activities. I talked to Scott as much as I could about the trophies not meaning Kathleen was better than he was — and still Scott's longing prevailed.

Then came Scott's birthday. I can still remember the burst of joy he expressed as he opened the gift from his sister: A giant trophy which read, "SCOTT MCDANIEL, For Always Being So Enthusiastic." Kathleen had called a friend's dad who owned a trophy store and this was their gift to Scott.

Today, Scott's room is filled with trophies. Right in the middle of them is one which he values most of all — a gift of love from his sister and his friend.

Your child's needs and wants may not be realistic. Lessons of acceptance are difficult ones. It is important to honor the feelings — and in some cases, grant a wish. Your child's needs and wants are not yours. Don't judge the request, just deal with it the best you can.

UNDERSTANDING IS OFTEN TAUGHT
THROUGH COMMUNICATION

> Essential Ingredients:
> Patience • Compassion • Gentleness

Remember: Your child's perception of the world is being formed. What you say in words and actions is inscribed inside of him/her in indelible ink.

Kathleen was sitting outside our front door one day. She was nine years old. Her arms were folded by her chest and she was crying. I went out and sat next to her. For awhile, I said nothing nor did I touch her. Finally, she said, "I hate (name)! I'd like to punch out her lights!" Still I said nothing. She continued, "She thinks she is so perfect. Doesn't she realize what she says can hurt people's feelings? Why doesn't she care about hurting other people, Mom?" I thought for a minute and said the only thing I could think of, "Maybe she isn't being taught to be kind at home." Kathleen's head snuggled under my arm and we just sat there in the silence of our understanding.

Scott arrived in life with a mission no one had to teach him: to care about everyone. He would sit in the "way back" of our station wagon and ardently wave to everybody. One time, he crawled clear up to the front, leaned over the seat saying, "Mom, I waved and waved at a man. He looked at me but he didn't wave. Why didn't he wave?" My eyes met his in the rearview mirror as I said, "Maybe he just isn't a waver, Scott." He thought about it and returned to his post. From that time on, I could tell when someone didn't wave back as I'd hear him say, "Oh, oh, guess he/she isn't a waver!"

If I had labeled the person by saying, "He must be a (jerk)," I'd have missed a chance to teach about differences. Some people were not brought up to be friendly. It is an individual choice to be friendly. Scott was less likely to stop giving out his caring if he learned to honor differences.

I remember someone telling me that she passed Scott every morning as he was riding his bicycle to school. Though he was always friendly, this person reported her delight with his comment that morning, "Beautiful day today, isn't it?" I don't ask Scott to be friendly. I model being friendly and have not dampened his natural tendency to talk to others.

ASKING QUESTIONS

> Essential Ingredients:
> Patience • Perseverance • Kindness

Remember: Your reality is seldom the same as your child's. Many children are very literal.

When Kathleen was in fourth grade and Scott was in second grade they both took gymnastics. Neither one of them liked the experience. All I heard was grumps and groans about going to sessions with no information as to the problem.

Ten years later, we were talking about the time they took gymnastics and hated it. Kathleen piped up with, "We were in a carpool and had to change in the back of the car. The boys tried to watch and it was awful." Scott said, "They never explained that you had to work hard to get your muscles strong so you could safely do the fun things. All they did was get mad at you if you asked a question."

I couldn't believe it! The answer to my question as to why they didn't like gymnastics was answered ten years after the fact. When I asked them why they hadn't told me, they both said, together, "You didn't ask the question for that answer!"

Children seldom know the answer to your question, "Why?" Try instead: "Tell me what it is about gymnastics that bothers you the most," or to get it off of them, "If I went to gymnastics, what might be the worst thing for me?"

Most children will respond to a question about what is bothering them with, "I don't know," or "Nothing." Try instead, "It seems as if you are upset about something. You might not want to talk about it right now, but if you do I will listen." Neither one of my children can talk about something when they are upset. Both of them will talk about their feelings when they can. I like to get into something right away and clear it up so it is over. It is important that I respect this difference in our approach to handling troubles — otherwise, one problem turns into two!

"Why did you do that?" seldom gets an answer. "Tell me what was going on when you chose to do that," is an invitation to work on something together. Or try: "I don't have a picture about what happened. Tell me your version of the fight you had with Kathleen." (*Note: Saying "your version" recognizes that there are two sides to every fight.*)

Choose the words in your questions carefully.

BE CAREFUL NOT TO INVALIDATE FEELINGS

> Essential Ingredients:
> Listening • Not Judging • Communication

**Remember: Feeling feelings is important. Some actions
need to be contained and corrected.**

Every human being experiences a myriad of feelings. Feelings are
indicative of the way we think, how we perceive life, and the reason we
make the choices we do. Feeling feelings is an endangered art among
most human beings. It is very difficult to teach your children to
reorganize and feel feelings if you do not feel your own.

My children have been encouraged to feel any feelings that they
might have. Choosing appropriate behavior around those feelings is an
area in which I've provided continual guidance. If your child feels angry
and breaks a window, the feeling of anger was all right — breaking the
window was not.

Teaching children to allow their feelings and to deal with them
constructively is not an easy process. The results of your efforts in this
fragile area will become obvious, especially when they become teenagers.

When Scott was going to a dance for the first time, he was gray
with fear. Had I said, "Are you nervous?" it would have pointed out a
fact he was trying to hide. If I said, "Hey, man, there's nothing to be
afraid of!" I would have invalidated his feelings. Instead, I said, "You'll
probably be surprised to know that I can remember as far back as the first
time I went to dance. It was weird because I wasn't worried about the
dancing part — I was worried about what you say to a boy when his face
is only a foot from yours. Seems to me the best thing is to think of some
things to say ahead of time. What are some questions or topics you could
talk about since school is just starting?" He suggested asking about the
summer, what teacher she had, and whether she liked being back in
school. Armed with the safety of having thought about a scary situation
ahead of time, Scott's nervousness subsided.

In my workshops on self-esteem, I have seen again and again,
adults who close down and fail to communicate with each other because
one or the other invalidates feelings.

If you honor your own feelings, it is easier to honor the feelings of
those around you.

WORKING THROUGH FEELINGS

> Essential Ingredients:
> Courage • Trust • Communication

Remember: Children are taught to trust and work with their feelings according to your response to them.

At eleven, Scott decided he wanted to go to Wilderness Survival Camp in Wyoming. The night before he left on his enormous adventure, reality and fear struck simultaneously. We had the following conversation:

S: "Do you know how hard it is to leave your family?"

M: "Probably the hardest thing you've ever done."

S: "Uh-huh (crying) Do you think I'll ever stop crying?"

M: "Sure. It's OK to cry — and best to cry until you don't need to any more. Don't cut off your tears."

S: "Now you're crying. I'm glad you're sad, too (tears). Then I'm not doin' all the missing."

M: "No way will you do all the missing, pal."

S: "Would you rub my back and give me a lecture so I'll get bored and go to sleep?"

M: (laughing) "Sure."

Had I told Scott there was nothing to be afraid of, I would have negated his feelings and been lying. I was a little concerned about his going as well, so he would have sensed that I wasn't telling the truth. It wasn't my job to paint a glorious picture about his first trip away from home. My job was to honor his feelings of fear.

The next morning, he got up, got dressed, ate breakfast and walked onto the airplane with his friend. Though his eyes were wide and his shoulders rose and fell as he took deep breaths, he crossed over his fear and went to camp.

When Kathleen was in her first play, she was terrified the day of the performance. Her biggest fear was that she'd forget her lines and make a fool out of herself. I didn't tell her that her feelings were foolish and she'd be OK. I'm not a fortune teller. What we did instead was to talk about things she could do to keep her mind busy so she wouldn't worry. Taking lots of deep breaths helped give air to her nervous body. We played a card game in the afternoon and I didn't talk about the play at all. The play finally came, and Kathleen didn't forget a line.

When the truth is spoken, surrounded with kindness, children call on their own resources to go through the moment and face their fear. Children who face rather than run away from fears develop emotional muscle to withstand the many pressures over the years.

EMPATHIZE WITH YOUR CHILDREN

> Essential Ingredients:
> Listening • Compassion • Patience

Remember: There can be a difference between loving your child and having your child feel loved. Try to "walk in each child's moccasins."

When Scott decided to go to Wilderness Survival Camp. I talked to him the day before he left (as reality was beginning to dawn on him). "What is the scariest thought you have about doing this right now?"

Scott replied, "What do you say to a bus load of kids you don't even know, for four hours?"

"Well," I began, "you can always ask where each person is from — and — if you want to open a real can of worms, ask if anyone besides you didn't sleep last night. My guess is that you are not alone in being afraid. So the subject of fear comes up, there will be plenty of talk, and you will all be closer because for your sharing."

Note: Scott did the above, and said everyone talked for hours. One kid said he cried all night and they all laughed, sharing their fears.

Telling a child who is afraid of something that there is nothing to be afraid of invalidates their feeling. How do you know what is scary for that child?

Scott would start walking down to his bedroom at night. At the door, his imagination would remind him there was a creature down there that ate kids his size, so he would become immobilized in front of the door. His father might have said, "Go ahead, Scott, there's nothing to be afraid of." Or even worse: "Don't be a coward, son, go on down there!"

When Scott froze, he noticed he was afraid. Now, the person he wants most to think he is wonderful (Dad), called him a coward. It costs nothing to get up, walk down the hall saying, "Remember the time you were afraid to ride the bicycle? You've got that handled now — this will change, too."

Fears are private things. A requirement for changing any fear is to not take in outside judgment or to judge yourself. Most often, change comes from communication, new experiences and time.

PARENTAL ATTITUDES

MAKING MISTAKES

> Essential Ingredients:
> Modeling • Patience • Sense of Humor

Remember: No one can go through a day without making mistakes. Learning to accept mistakes is the bridge to learning from them.

Think of yourself as a coach. You are teaching your child a myriad of skills in order to master living effectively in a very complex time. New techniques require training and room for mistakes.

When a child is afraid to make a mistake withholding is the result. A "shy" child might be withholding for fear of making a mistake. Fear causes the part of your brain where reasoning occurs to shut down. Therefore fear of making a mistake usually results in more mistakes.

If your child puts a dish on the sink rather than in the dishwasher, say to that child, "Scott, the dish goes into the dishwasher when you are finished using it. Please go put your dish in the dishwasher right now. Next time, put it there rather than on the sink."

Scott wanted to challenge this rule. He left a dish on the sink after I had used the words above. I got his bicycle out of the garage, rode to the next block where he was playing ball and said to him quietly, "Dishes go in the dishwasher. You left a dish on the sink so I want you to go home and put it into the dishwasher now, please." Even though he promised to do it the minute he got home, I insisted he go home immediately to complete his job. When he asked to use his bicycle I refused. An angry boy of eight stormed home — but dishes somehow got into the dishwasher thereafter — because I showed him one of the most essential ingredients of parenthood: FOLLOW-THROUGH.

An effective consequence is to do something on "their time": If the toys weren't picked up in the den, they need to be put away before watching television. If clothes were left strewn around, they need to be put away before it's OK to go outside and play. Consequences need to relate to the problem. I see no point in taking away television for forgetting to bring your skateboard inside one night. Take the skateboard away for a day instead.

Children who are taught to work with their mistakes trust themselves more and tend to be more productive human beings.

MISTAKES ARE THE WAY YOU LEARN

> Essential Ingredients:
> Separate Child & Behavior • Patience • Trust

Remember: No one is doing life perfectly — mistakes are a natural part of life.

In the research being done on successful companies and what makes them tick, businesses that not only allow but encourage mistakes as a process of discovery are among the most successful ones. This is a difficult concept for most individuals as we've been taught to avoid mistakes at all costs.

When a coach is working with an athlete, there is a continuous process of correction going on — with the coach giving information in the form of feedback and the athlete practicing to make the necessary changes.

You are a coach for your children. Their learning is a process which sometimes takes time.

Kathleen was nine when she brought in her first low grade on a paper. Stomping into the den where I was reading, she tossed a page onto the desk stating, "You're 'spose to sign that!" Her body language told me she was not pleased with the paper. I looked and saw a "D" clearly marked at the top.

M: "What did you learn?"
K: "Well, if I'd learned something I wouldn't have gotten a D!"
M: "What did you learn?"
K: "Can't you see there is a D on the top of that paper?"
M: "Kathleen, what did you learn?"
K: "Well...I learned that I have to study for her tests, and I can't fake it in this class, and I have to read the book."
M: (Signing the paper) "Here's your paper."
K: "Aren't you going to punish me?"
M: "Why would I when you learned so much?"

If the child needs assistance with a subject get help right away. Getting hopelessly lost in school is the end of the world to a child's sense of self-esteem. Few children willingly accept the idea of a tutor, and a tutor might save your child from escalating problems in school.

TEACH TEACHING NOT CORRECTING

> Essential Ingredients:
> Patience • Understanding • Love

Remember: Your perception of how something needs to be done and your child's perception can be miles apart.

You are the coach and your children are in training for living independent lives. Part of that training is to take care of their own things as well as assisting with the over-all care of the home.

Something that is simple in your mind may not be simple to your small child. Putting blocks into a box can be very frustrating if the box is small and the job needs to be done in a certain way. Maybe a cardboard carton with wrapping paper around it would be an appropriate container for toys. If certain boxes are for certain kinds of toys, you begin to teach lessons about order.

When a child is big enough to make his/her bed, teach how to make it and then let their version be good enough. Re-doing something a child does gives a very clear message of incompetence. If you want the job done better next time, assist with the bed making the next morning as a teaching, not a reprimanding project.

Teach how to put soap in a rag and wipe it off — then how to rinse the rag and put it back where it belongs.

Teach a child how to set the table, and let it be OK if the fork is in the wrong place for awhile.

Teach a child how to hammer a nail into a board (and be sure to teach exactly which boards need nails!)

Doing something together is much more fun than doing it alone. Clean the bathtub together. Clean the refrigerator together. When there is a spill, clean it together (which also teaches taking responsibility for mistakes). Vacuum together. Dust together. If you are wiping the door, give the child the "way-down-bottom" part and you do the rest.

Teach your children how to cook. Food comes in pre-packaged form but few young people can afford that kind of food. Teach them how to cook so they can feed themselves.

LISTENING TO YOUR CHILD

> Essential Ingredients:
> Time • Awareness • Patience

Remember: One of the most precious gifts you can give your children is the feeling that they have been heard.

A child once defined a grandmother as "Someone who has time to listen." When children do not feel heard (notice I emphasize *feeling heard* rather than *are listened to*) they go inward and either become isolationist or seek inappropriate friendships to fill their void.

You can't always listen to your child—especially in those years from 2 through 6 where life is an endless question or comment. It is important that you teach your child that there are times you can listen and times you can not. I can't cook dinner and listen, so I take my child into another room, give him or her something to do and set a timer saying, "I can't fix dinner and listen at the same time. When this bell rings, I will be finished with what I am doing. When I hear this bell, I'll come and listen to you."

Explaining **why** I couldn't listen is essential as I want to teach through understanding. From understanding comes cooperation and compassion.

Some guidelines for listening are: (1) Don't give advice, (2) Don't interrupt with a story about the good ol' days and how it was for you, and (3) Physically get down on their level whenever possible (or raise him/her to yours).

If your child says something like, "I think they should shoot the man who shot those people!" and you are against violence, stop! Don't react! If you interrupt a child's thought with a lecture of your own, there is very little chance that he/she will share thoughts with you again. You want to know what the child is thinking about. Say, "Tell me more about that." You might reflect back what you heard, "You are really angry that someone hurt other people and you want to hurt him back."

If the child asks what you think, talk without indicating (with words or body language) that you think the child's thought is stupid. It might be wise to talk about your feelings later: "I was thinking about what you said at dinner the other night, and I am against killing someone for killing someone else. It just doesn't add up with me. Also, we have no way of knowing everything that happened to cause the problem. Those are just my thoughts." Listen to your child. Listen! Listen! Listen! Listen! Listen! Listen! Listen! !

OPENLY EXPRESS APPRECIATION FOR YOUR CHILD

> Essential Ingredients:
> Trust Yourself • Commitment • Communication

Remember: What seems obvious to you may not be obvious to your child.

I've worked with "at risk" children and have found that too often parents assume the child has the same reasoning faculty as they do. It was in a drug center that a teenage boy said, "My parents don't give a damn about me. They are never around." When confronted with that information, the parents said they had both taken extra work loads in order to bring in extra money for the boy's schooling. **THOSE PARENTS HAD NOT TOLD THE BOY WHAT THEY WERE DOING OR WHY.** So that family ended up in major crisis over a simple misconception.

It is such a complex time to be living in this world. You cannot appreciate your children too much. Be certain that your appreciation is expressed in every way you can:

- Leave notes when you aren't home saying when you expect to return.
- Leave a thank you note (for picking up a jacket by the door) on that child's bed, or verbally acknowledge that act.
- Moms **and** Dads, hug your child good morning. Hug and kiss your child good night.
- Say, "I'm suppose to love you because I'm your mother. (father) What I want you to know is that I like you, too." (Never say this unless it is the truth!)

My Kathleen loves her brother and is always open to assisting him with his life. One time, after she had spent several hours working with him on one of his projects, I leaned in the door and said, "I love your brother and I love you, thanks for spending time working with him."

I sometimes open Kathleen's bed (I'd do it for Scott but I'm afraid to go into his pit alone at night!), and put a note on her pillow, "Hope you had fun, sleep well."

When Kathleen was in finals at college (and living at home), I put a note on her steering wheel, "Do your best today, it's good enough. I love you! Mom."

GIVE CHILDREN LOTS OF LOVE NOTES

> Essential Ingredients:
> Love • Time • Thought

Remember: Children thrive on encouragement.

It is a harsh world, this world we have created. The life of our children is nothing like our own childhood. There is no way to protect their innocence or to keep them from too much of some kinds of information at small ages.

You cannot love your children too much. You can do things that look loving but really aren't. That kind of love is harmful. Really, truly loving children in a way that is felt is an antidote for the many ills of society.

When Kathleen was small, I put poems, drawings and messages on her napkins for her daily lunch. I laughed when one mother called me saying, "Would you quit sending the napkins with drawings, now all the children want napkins with drawings." I didn't quit. In her closet is a bag of napkins which Kathleen has never thrown away.

I am a professional public speaker, so from time-to-time, do some traveling. My two children always leave a message somewhere in my suitcase. One time, I thought they had forgotten because unpacking didn't uproot a message. In the middle of a talk, I was reading things that children have written and there was a note which said, "Hello mother! We figure you will be tired when you get home, so we are going to fix your dinner. We love you!"

When Scott went to Wilderness Survival School, I put endless notes in everything from shoes to pockets. He said that finding them helped him to survive his homesickness.

Sometimes, when I am wearily headed for bed (long after the troops have gone to sleep), I'll find my bed turned down with a "Night Mom, I love you!" note from a child. Over the years, I have turned down their beds when they were out, and left some hearts on a pillow, or a note. You teach best by modeling.

Love notes do not need to be store-bought. They do not need to be lengthy or eloquent. They need to be real. A love note from you has immeasurable value (Mom <u>and</u> Dad).

LOVING REMINDERS TEACH WITHOUT HARM

> Essential Ingredients:
> Sense of humor • Perseverance • Compassion

Remember: You are the coach and learning is a process that takes time.

Each of my children has a wonderful sense of humor. So do I. We have turned many situations that could have become a battle into something fun by appropriately using that humor.

• Scott and I both tend to be a little dramatic. We are constantly in danger of overdoing our part. One morning, he tramped into the kitchen ranting and raving, "I don't want to go to school, I hate to fix breakfast, I don't know what to wear, and what's even worse, this is only Monday! Why was I born, anyway?" It wasn't his words so much as the extreme body action that was entertaining. I leaned against the wall and watched. At the very height of his drama, he turned his head and got that sheepish look on his face, saying, "Over-acting again, huh?"

"One of your best, Robert!" I lovingly responded.
He shrugged his shoulders and went on with his day.

Scott and I had previously agreed that whenever I call him "Robert" (for Robert Redford) or he calls me "Sarah" (for Sarah Bernhart), it is a loving message that overacting is in progress.

• When Kathleen went through her imperial stage, Scott called her "Your Majesty." He was so blatantly behind his joke that she couldn't keep from laughing.

• In one of our mother-son talks, I told Scott of my concern that he and I are somehow emotionally bonded so we tend to rise and fall emotionally with each other. I wanted us to work on letting each other feel our own feelings without influencing the other person's feelings. As I left, his voice followed, "Thanks, E!" My heart burst as I said, "You're welcome...T!"

• One day, Scott, going into his macho stage (which I fear is permanent), strutted up to me saying, "Listen here, woman! From now on you will call me Maverick or you will call me nothing!" For weeks, I called him "Nothing."

• Humor used on both sides builds incredible bonds of trust and gives you wondrous stories for your heart.

USE NOTES FOR REMINDING

> Essential Ingredients:
> Sense of Humor • Time • Patience

Remember: You are the coach and changing behavior is a process of learning.

Children have a way of turning a deaf ear to constant reminders (No, your child isn't the only one who does that!). Notes help you keep your balance in a world that seems unending in its demands for your patience. Notes can help children remember things.

On the dishwasher: *I am the world's greatest dishwasher, but I need your dishes to prove it!*

On the ice cube trays: *These ice cubes do not clone themselves, please refill.*

On the door of the messy room: *The sanitation department was here and declared this space a national disaster. Please remedy this situation by 5:00 P.M.*

On the floor as they come in the door: *Go immediately to the kitchen, put your breakfast dishes into the dishwasher then get a snack. Thank you! The Management.*

On the jacket by the door: *I belong in your room, please put me there.*

The whole family can discuss areas for possible improvement and think of appropriate signs to be made. Be aware that parents might get signs in return: Having given a talk and gotten caught in traffic, I was an hour late in getting home. There was a note on the floor: "Since our mother doesn't love us any more, we are leaving home. (over) Just kidding! We have gone to get some dinner."

Once there was a note on the pantry door, "I am supposed to hold food for teenagers. No teenager would be caught dead eating the stuff in here!" It was a note about going to the market.

Note on my car steering wheel: *"Thanks Mom for getting some Chocolate Mint Ice Cream when you go to the store today! I love you! Kathleen."*

Life is too serious too soon for these tiny humans that are under our care. Enjoy them! Much too soon, you will be left with the memories of the way they were.

DO YOU ALWAYS NEED TO BE RIGHT?

> Essential Ingredients
> Humility • Speak the Truth • A Sense of Humor

Remember: What you model is what you teach. Teaching how to handle mistakes is best done by handling them well.

I've heard many teenagers say, "The problem with my dad (or mom) is he/she always has to be right."

No one is always right. Always being right is a mathematical impossibility as a human being and a totally illogical goal for a parent. In addition, if you have to be perfect, you give your children an impossible role model to emulate.

Mistakes are a natural part of living. It is important that you handle an error calmly and without unnecessary drama.

Let's say you yell at your child only to find out later that the child had nothing to do with the situation. It is easy to grovel or to act imperial in such a situation. The truth needs to be spoken, nothing else. "You know, I got a little carried away there. I'm sorry about yelling, and I'm really sorry that I blamed you for something you didn't even do. I wish I could do it over, but I can't. Next time, I will remember to ask before I accuse." The child who has had time to build on his/her resentment may want to vent some anger, "Well, you didn't have to yell and scream about it !" This is not the time to grovel. Say, "I wish I could do it over. What else do you want to say so we can forget the whole thing and get on with being friends?"

If your child starts calling names or venting anger in a way that is difficult to handle, simply get it back on course with, "No name calling. Just tell me what you are feeling, please." People have been taught to name call, not to identify and state feelings. It is an endless challenge to teach children to speak about their true feelings.

Your children will teach you as much or more as you will teach them. Respect their wisdom by being honest about your imperfection without burdening them with it. You're doing your best — your best is good enough.

SPEND ONE-TO-ONE TIME WITH EACH CHILD

> Essential Ingredients
> Time • Listening Skills • Love

Remember: Spending time with each child is a irrefutable message of love.

I was the speaker when my daughter graduated from high school. One of my messages concerned the times we as parents had built walls between us and our children, when we meant to build bridges. When you have a graduating senior it is too late to spend the kind of time with that child that can build bridges.

Nothing you are doing, including your job, is more important than being with your children. A horrifying statistic says that as little as four and a half minutes a day is the average time a child talks to his/her parents—and that two and a half minutes of that time is spent in correcting. That leaves two minutes a day for morals, values and "Oh, by the way, I love and care about you." Pitted against the messages of television and the world in which your child walks daily, **that is not enough time!**

Take one child to breakfast, lunch or dinner once a week. Go for a walk together. Go somewhere away from the family and do something where talking is invited.

You don't know what to say? Small children like to imagine things: "If you had a magic wand, what would you do with it?" Older children sometimes respond to: "Life was different when I was your age, what's the hardest thing for you about being (age)?" I ask my children to comment on our relationship with: "I've been really busy lately and pretty preoccupied, how are we doing — you and I?" Sometimes, it is fun to ask, "What if I were a Martian visiting planet Earth and I was (your child's age). What would I be like, what would I need to know?"

Please remember that defensiveness, lectures and tons of free advice insure a response to every question in the future will be: "I don't know." If you are given some information about you or something you did which is hard to take in, say: "Thanks for your honesty. I'll think about that."

When grown-ups take time to be with children and create a safe space where the truth may be spoken, it is a bridge of unimaginable strength and value for each of you.

BE PLAYFUL — ENJOY YOUR CHILDREN!

> Essential Ingredients:
> Sense of Humor • Time • Imagination

Remember: If you make being a grown up look like its no fun, why will your children want to become one?

Life is a serious affair filled with opportunities, choices and consequences. On your worst parenting day, the time you have with your children will go too fast. Have fun with your children!

- It's one thing to push a small child in a swing and quite another if you swing with your child.

- You may not be a great basketball player, but if you make even a feeble attempt to shoot an occasional basket there is a bridge built between the two of you.

- Leaving appropriate cartoons masking-taped to the door or giving a crazy card for no particular reason keeps your child's and your own perspective in order — and lets life be fun!

- If you get sick of questions like, "What's for dinner?" followed by gagging sounds, try responding with crazy answers: Tyrannosaurus burgers, stork eggs and...."

When my children were little I wrote notes on the napkins that were in their lunches. When Scott was 16, I put some dinosaur cookies in his lunch with a "memories" note on his napkin. He came home smiling and gave me a hug. I asked him if he was embarrassed opening that part of his lunch. "Nah, the guys wanted to know what it was, then we all talked about how much we liked dinosaurs when we were kids."

The first time Kathleen went away on a sizable trip I wrote endless mothering notes on cards and tucked them into her clothes. She had many laughs finding such reminders as: "Brushed your teeth?" or "Braces need rubberbands, right?" or "Miss my cooking, right?"

Enjoy your children today. Teach them to find joy and laughter in each day. Teach them those things by modeling them. All of life is a matter of attitude and perspective.

BUYING EQUAL GIFTS FOR CHILDREN

> Essential Ingredients
> Communication • Unconditional Love • Trust

Remember: Children who feel loved do so because of the way they are treated not by the gifts that are given.

I have worked with many a rich kid in a drug center or in Juvenile Hall who had everything that money could buy but didn't feel loved. What you give your children in terms of the gifts you buy can never be measured against the gift of really caring about the development and well- being of that child.

Some families give equal gifts. If the father is on a business trip, each child is brought a present. If the mother finds something for one child while shopping, she gets busy buying token gifts for the other children. I don't do that. It's too expensive and it isn't an honest gift. I think children know about such things as honest gifts.

When I come home with a new T-shirt for Scott, I just give it to him. Even a sentence like, "I didn't have time to get anything for you, Kathleen," builds the idea that I should give equally. Children have different needs at different times. Boys are far less interested (over-all) in clothes than girls seem to be, and a boy's wardrobe is far less complicated to form than a girl's. Equal spending becomes absurd.

When the children were little, one might ask, "How come you got something for him and not for me?" That's a fair question. I answered, "I saw this and thought of Scott, so I got it for him. Maybe he will share it with you when he gets finished checking it out." Nothing more needs be said. If the child persists, simply tell the truth, "Sometimes I see something just right for you. Sometimes I see something just right for Scott. Sometimes, he will get a new thing that I bring home and sometimes, you will. Today, I just got something for Scott."

The bottom line is not to give gifts as a measurement of love. A human being values being loved for him/herself. Unconditional love means to love someone no matter what his/her actions might be. When you do not like a certain behavior and still like/love the child, that child **feels** loved. When this kind of parenting occurs, unequal receiving becomes irrelevant to each of your children.

DEALING WITH ILLNESS

> Essential Ingredients:
> Patience • Compassion • Detachment

Remember: Worry does not help your child either physically or mentally.

It is perfectly natural to feel alarm when your child becomes ill. For most parents, there is a tendency to over- react.

Children can be taught very early to escape from life through illness or to become hypochondriacs for the attention they need. Correspondingly, loving a child who is ill is the most powerful medicine you can provide. Holding a sick child has unfathomable value. The challenge is: to care about the child's wellness, not to become hysterical or melodramatic, and not to ignore the child because you don't know what to do.

Bringing a sick child lots of presents can become a reward that backfires. Giving a sick child a gift that assists with the healing process (something to do, something to hold onto) is valuable. A child who does not feel he/she is getting enough attention may resort to illness (real or imaginary) in order to get your love.

One night, both babies had the flu — one or the other was constantly vomiting or pooping. Changing sheets got to be a routine activity. The washing machine chugged all night long. Dick and I met in the hallway, he with clean sheets, I with newly soiled ones, "Wizard night, huh?" I groaned, leaning against the wall. Probably more as a reaction to exhaustion than my humor, we both fell on the floor laughing.

Sometimes, especially for teenagers, making the day school is missed more boring than school is a great incentive towards a speedy recovery. This is best accomplished by banning any television watching during the day.

Being sure that reasonable homework is sent home from school keeps your child mindful of his/her responsibilities. If the school sends an unreasonable amount of homework following a lengthy illness (more than 3 days) talk to the teacher(s) about the unnecessary stress created by such an obligation. I watched my high school age son trash a whole semester of grades because he couldn't catch up in work or comprehension after being quite ill. If you have a high school student who has been ill, temporary tutoring helps. Also, make some sort of an agreement (see page 30) towards a study schedule which allows him/her to catch up. Help your teenager to reconcile time lost from illness.

HUG YOUR BOYS AND GIRLS

> Essential Ingredients:
> Trust • Compassion • Understanding

Remember: Children and adults need nurturing.

In a world where sexuality is so distorted, there has been an increasing fear among parents about touching their children. When is it appropriate and when is it not to hug or kiss your child? I think the answer is an individual one, and is dependent upon your ability to read and respect your children's needs.

Little boys do not need a handshake from their father, they need a hug. Sitting in Dad's lap is just as important as sitting in Mother's lap. There are too many emotionally crippled men in the world who never once heard their father say, "I love you." Even if you think you will choke to death if you try, say it anyway. As parents you are the center of the world to your infant. Love is the protective shield in which your child puts him/herself while learning to be safe in his/her own life.

There are stages when children become independent and don't want to be hugged or kissed. There is no mystery as to when that time arrives, it is announced by the sound, "Yuck!" following your hug or kiss. It is at these times that a substitute for hugging can be fun. A substitute hug honors the child's struggle for independence: A high five or other hand signal can be your own private "I love you" message. With a girl you can learn the hand signing for "I love you" and give it to each other. Little boys do not like to have their hair ruffled by an adult.

Women are looked to as the nurturers and often the boys are brought up as if they have a switch which circumvents their need to be nurtured. From about nine or ten on, some boys do not seem to like to cuddle, so nurturing may take a different form.

Scott's Uncle Jim was visiting recently. When Scott came into the room, Jim offered his hand. Scott pushed his hand aside, and hugged him saying, "You forget who my mother is!" At seventeen Scott has enough self-confidence to offer a hug when it is appropriate.

Each day I think about how much I love my children. I tell them "I love you" in words and appropriate touching.

THE ROLE OF THE FATHER

> Essential Ingredients:
> Commitment • Compassion • Communication

Remember: As the adult male in your family, you are helping to mold your children's feelings towards both the same and opposite sex.

In my era, children often heard the phrase, "You wait until your father comes home. He will spank you for what you have done!" So, the father, tired from a day or work and totally out of touch with the problem that occurred, became the disciplinarian.

I think consequences are to be given by either or both parents. I feel strongly that situations which are dealt with as they occur have much more value in terms of teaching children to modify behavior.

It is difficult to come home from the mental/physical stress of work and have any desire whatsoever to play with or even talk to small children. Hugs and excitement when daddy comes home is a wonderful way to be greeted. If you, as the father, need some space when you get home, you need to state that in words everyone understands: "I want to talk to and play with you. Right now, I need to change my clothes and take a few minutes to rest up from my day. We will talk at dinner and play after dinner."

If the father talks about hating work all the time, there is little chance the children will get a favorable idea about going to work.

The mother, who has had the children all day with no breaks, really appreciates a husband who takes the children for some one-to-one time. Changing diapers, feeding babies, giving baths, reading stories, playing games, going to the park, coloring or painting are all things that both parents need to share.

In most homes, a man spends comparatively less time with the children than the woman does. Research has proven time and time again that the kind of time you spend in fathering is far more important that the amount of time. And, as a parent who is living with two young adults, I remind you that the time you have with your children is very, very short.

Those of us who were blessed with fathers who invested time in our lives know how preciously we hold those memories. What none of us realized was how much of our picture of ourself and others (especially men) came from the time we spent with dad.

LET YOUR BOY CRY APPROPRIATELY

> Essential Ingredients:
> Kindness • Time • Compassion

Remember: Your son has the same feelings as your daughter. Men who stuff their feelings have many emotional and physical problems.

A little boy falls down and scrapes his knee—it is bleeding and it hurts. Too often the father is heard to say, "Don't cry son, be a man." Your boy is not a man, he is a child who is learning to feel feelings and to respond to life. Telling him to stuff his feelings will damage his lifetime sense of self-trust. Boys can cry. Maybe if we let more boys cry there will be less men who emotionally numb out so they can't feel their feelings.

My sixteen year old son, Scott, doesn't cry easily but he does let his eyes water without embarrassment. I was watching the movie, "Mr. Smith Goes to Washington," which my children bought for me. Scott came through the room, looked at the TV and asked, "Are you crying, yet?" Then he sat down to watch the ending with me and while he was checking out my tears I noticed his eyes were moist. I value having a son who dares to care about people.

Scott and I got caught in traffic while going shopping one day. A major accident was the cause of our delay. As we rounded the corner, sitting next to a bandaged man laying in a stretcher was a small boy with tear-filled eyes. The boy looked up, and Scott waved in a simple gesture of caring. I began to cry. Scott's hand took mine and when I looked at him, there were tears in his eyes. That moment of shared caring is an indelible imprint on both of our hearts.

When Scott and I go to a movie and I am welling up with tears, his hand touches mine. How does he know I am about to cry? Yes, he knows me — and he allows himself to feel his own emotions as well.

Disappointed at his grades, Scott began to cry. "I'm sorry!" he kept saying, and I replied, "Don't be sorry, feel your feelings, they're OK."

Using tears as a means of controlling adults and having tears as an expression of feelings are two different things. A child who over-cries is having his/her own brand of temper tantrum. Love the child and stop the behavior by saying, "When you are through crying about this, come find me and we'll talk." Then leave the drama to the actor. Behavior that is not rewarded will change.

CHILDREN IN ORGANIZED SPORTS

> Essential Ingredients:
> Integrity • Communication • Humility

Remember: The value of sports is to keep the body fit and teach children important personal skills.

Back there in the good ol' days, young men went off to do their tour of duty in the military. Today we send our sons to a place of equal jeopardy — organized sports. (Even worse, we now send our daughters as well.)

As a child who was eleven pounds at birth and very coordinated Scott was destined to be in sports. At sixteen Scott is six foot four inches tall. The question he is most often asked is, "Do you play basketball?"

Indeed, Scott plays basketball. I went to a varsity summer league game last night. Afterwards, I walked home trying to release my anger at the emotional abuse he and his friends received for two hours of what is otherwise called "play". If someone made a mistake, he was immediately taken out of the game. Any basic educator knows that when a person is pressured and is afraid to make a mistake, a mistake is inevitable. The argument is that we make "boys into men" by beating them to death verbally and by punishing anything but perfection. BALONEY! I saw no encouragement or specific training to do better — just endless reprimand. And if we allow these standards to prevail in our schools, what will we have in the end? Is a society that values winning over respect and support one in which we will all survive? I think not.

A few years back, my children both played soccer. I was amazed at the anger some parents verbalized over a single child's performance in a "game." I saw children's self-esteem squashed, hearts broken, spirits trashed over a point made or not made in a game which does not matter in the over-all scheme of things.

Parents of children in sports who are abusive please note: When pressured into performing for the sake of pleasing a parent, a child's hostility rate steadily increases. Too many teenagers who commit suicide do so because they can't be good enough. Good enough for what? (Or is it good enough for whom?)

It's hard to think about what really matters when our egos get involved. A child who is good in sports has so much pressure to excel. At the very least, doing your best and having fun needs to be the primary criteria for all sports — and parents who **need** their children to be sport heros need to stay home.

GOING TO SCHOOL

Essential Ingredients:
Trust • Communication • Integrity

Remember: Accelerated learning at too young an age can be detrimental to that child.

Learning specialists are telling us that there is more to having the creative arts as a vital part of learning than just letting children have fun. Different children learn in different ways. In learning there are many ingredients: experiencing, thinking, reasoning and intuitive responses are equally valuable to memorizing facts. We are turning out too many whiz kids who have no compassion because they had none for themselves as learners. There is too much stress among children in school. Some children begin their quest for good grades somewhere around kindergarten.

The brain takes in information and then puts it into compartments. It needs "down time" to do that (which is why some learning specialists discourage having a child listen to tapes during sleep time). Some children are kinesthetic learners, which is to say they need to be physically involved in the learning process to understand it. Some children hear <u>and</u> learn (auditory) and some children see <u>to</u> learn (visual). Every child needs to explore the different realms of learning that are afforded in art, music and creative play. More than balance, it is a matter of wholeness.

As an educator, I am appalled at the way our entire system has focused on the value of learning facts. Teachers now teach to accommodate tests. Test scores measure the success of a school. Children learn no life skills (except from teachers who teach in spite of the system). They learn to hate learning. Too many children are bored to death watching mindless lessons which require non-participatory attention and still bodies. And we wonder why there is a rebellion going on among children towards school!

Changing the school system will take time. PARENTS ARE AS MUCH AT FAULT FOR THE EMPHASIS ON LEARNING FACTS AS THE EDUCATORS. Encourage your children to participate in activities that supplement learning facts. Encourage your children to keep some of their time "free". Children learn important skills in their play. Encourage your child who doesn't do well in school. Most teachers are visual learners and presenters, so an auditory and kinesthetic learner has a very difficult time in our system.

Some children thrive in school, some do not. Help a struggling child to understand that the problem may be one of learning styles, not whether he/she is smart. Let it be OK to have a child who isn't a great student.

HELPING WITH SCHOOL WORK

> Essential Ingredients:
> Patience • Communication • Understanding

Remember: Your job is to assist your children with work, not to do it for them — or to go crazy trying.

Having been an elementary school teacher and a parent I have both perspectives on the value and possible harm in assisting children with their homework.

Your child goes to school (presumably) to learn how to assimilate facts, think and reason, manage time, learn to be sociable, understand the world around him/her and learn skills which assist in functioning successfully in the world. Time management is an essential part of your child having homework.

Parents who take over and do a project for a child give a significant message of ineptness to that child. It is also a conflict for the child to turn in a project and claim it is his/her own work. I still remember a speech my father took over and wrote for me in high school. The teacher came to me and asked that the text be entered into some competition. I refused, unable to give a reason. My ability to get into the college of my choice was dependent on my grade in that class. So I compromised and lied about having done the work myself. Yet I was unable to enter the speech in a contest. I'm forty-eight years old, and still remember the choice I made about one little assignment.

Parents who continually rescue the child who has "put-it -off-until-the-last-night-itis" teach that child to become a victim who needs a rescuer. Many adults are in victim-rescuer roles. Sometimes, letting your child "go under" is a more valuable lesson than saving him or her.

Teaching some children to write down their assignments and do them ahead of time seems impossible. Rather than nagging at the child set a consistent time (with no television) for doing school work. Consistency is the most valuable assistance a parent may give their child.

Some children need to go to Junior College rather than a big university. It is a scary world out there with pressures and demands that were incomprehensible in "our day." The national push to excel has over-ridden our need to raise children who have a strong sense of integrity and self- esteem. The result? Look at the harsh existence we have created all around us. I think there is much, much more to life than good grades and for some children, going to college. Junior college for some children is a safe place in which to be until they are able to make a different choice.

HELPING WITH SCHOOL WORK #2

Essential Ingredients: Patience • Creativity • Compassion

Remember: A child's job is to go to school. It is not your job to go back to school.

In my parenting workshops I have a section on teaching children how to memorize. I often say, "The trouble with your child having to learn the states and capitols is that now you have to learn them — again!"

There is great value, especially to the auditory and kinesthetic learners in having someone study or go over material with them. The value is lost, however, if the learning process creates a barrier between parent and child. Parents who get angry assisting with homework should not assist with homework.

There are some great memory tricks which children tend to pick up more readily than adults. The following is one way Scott remembered a state and its capitol:

Visualize a giant iceburg covered with hair. Above it is a huge pencil with lots of veins running through it. The pencil is writing the word "ya" on top of the hairy iceburg. Put them all together: Hairyburg (Harrisburg) Pencil-vein-ya. Visualize the picture. Harrisburg is the capitol of Pennsylvania.

If your child needs to learn a list of things in no special order, see if you can make a word from which all of the list may come: It is SLOWER to travel from the east to the west coast by covered wagon. The question is to name six things people brought in covered wagons. Write the word slower vertically and create a word for each letter:

S = soap
L = lantern
O = oxen
W = water
E = each person's personal things
R = rifle

Another way to memorize a list is to make a silly picture connecting all the pieces together. In the list above, the sillier the picture you create the easier it is to remember. Visualize the following: An oxen on a raft in the water, the raft is a giant bar of soap. The paddle is a huge rifle. Tied to the oxen's tail is a lantern, and the oxen has a giant earring in its nose.

Children can visualize and memorize things in a short time and remember those facts for years thereafter. It's fun!

HELPING CHILDREN WITH SCHOOL WORK #3

> Essential Ingredients:
> Patience • Communication • Perseverance

Remember: There is a difference between the words "assist" and "doing". Assisting children with homework can build a special bond. Doing for a child harms self-esteem.

Another way to assist children with memorizing is to use mneumonics (new-monics). In Junior High school (I remind you that I am currently 48), I needed to memorize five people who signed the Declaration of Independence. My "key" was to spell flags with a "j":

F = Franklin

L = Livingston

A = Adams

J = Jefferson

S = Sherman

In **Project Self-Esteem** we teach mneumonics as a means of learning all the Presidents in order. When you climb a mountain, you do so a little at a time. The first five Presidents are learned by isolating the first letter of each name (W, A, J, M, M). Using those letters, you make up a sentence that creates a silly picture for your mind: Whales Always Juggle Mice and Monkeys. Visualize a whale juggling mice and monkeys between its tail and spout. Write the first letter for each word in your silly picture and begin to learn a name with each letter (using flash cards for repetitive memorizing): W=Washington, A=Adams, J=Jefferson, M=Madison and M=Monroe (the two M's are in alphabetical order — or — you remember a "mad mon" for mad man). The picture gives you the letters and then you simply write the names. For the next five letters, you create another picture (in this case, using an animal since that's now the theme) and hook that picture to the one with the whale. Crazy pictures linked together in another crazy picture give a child an entertaining way of remembering something for a test — maybe forever.

Children who have difficulty memorizing spelling words need to get involved with the word. Have the child write each spelling word with a different colored felt pen. Have the child write the word and draw a picture using that word. Have the child write the word in finger paint. Have the child write the word in a sentence and then read the sentence aloud. Have the child write the word in a color, then say a sentence using the word; being dramatic with the sentence is fun, and lets the kinesthetic learner be involved for optimum learning. Switch ways of learning and see which works the best!

SUPPORTING CHILDREN'S CREATIVITY

> Essential Ingredients:
> Modeling • Communication • Creativity

Remember: Creativity can be enhanced or extinguished by parental responses.

One of my great concerns is that homes and schools tend to stifle the creativity of children. Our learning process thus becomes extremely mental. The result is compounding: the creation of a society that tends to depend on their minds and disregard feelings.

Rather than giving coloring books all the time, give a child a blank piece of paper on which to color or draw. Instead of asking a small child, "What is it?" which forces the child to give form to something that might be formless, say, "Tell me about your picture." A positive comment could be, "I like the way you used yellow, there."

Let children take blocks or Legos and build a "nothing". Invite creativity in the way they pick up toys, dress, play, and do their chores by turning tasks into miniature games.

Julie Johnson (who lives next door) and Kathleen decided if "mustard" was growing in the local fields, all they had to do was to cook some of those plants and they would have their own homemade creation. In the end, the pan needed to be thrown away. We talked about the advisability of checking in with a grown-up before you cook something — and I did not get angry with them. Their thought was a reasonable one. Their creativity was to be admired. Only their ability to know all facts was limited; that last part was the only place where we sought a remedy.

Every Christmas, when the children were small, we baked endless sugar cookies which they and their friend, Julie, covered with frosting plus little candy beads. Both the decorating of cookies and my kitchen could only be called creative! White or brown lunch bags got covered with paint, or glitter, or paint and glitter. They were the containers for the cookies which the children took around in a wagon to wish our neighbors a happy holiday.

The children dipped sponges into red and green paint to make designs on butcher paper. Each year we had homemade Christmas paper for wrapping gifts.

Christmas is about giving. Such projects taught Scott, Kathleen and Julie lessons about giving. Both their kindness as well as their creativity was appreciated by the neighbors. Me? I mostly appreciated when it was over — and it was always worth the trouble.

SUPPORTING CREATIVITY #2

> Essential Ingredients:
> Sense of humor • Awareness • Patience

Remember: Sometimes it is difficult to see the creativity in some of the more taxing activities your children choose.

My children always seemed to be the creative genius influence behind neighborhood horse-play; after awhile, we all stopped asking whose idea something was — everyone knew!

Julie and Kathleen decided they were bored. They were eating jelly beans, so they imagined that the green ones were energy pills which, when eaten, turned them into super-hyper humans. Throwing open the door to see what on earth all the noise was about, I saw two semi-hysterical tots bouncing back and forth from bed to bed, screaming and giggling. About the time I entered, they dropped to the floor in exhaustion. I laughed and left. Shortly, the same noise pattern resumed; having regained their breath, the two children had eaten another green jelly bean!

Julie and Kathleen vs Scott and his friend, Chris: There were water balloons, trash cans filled with water, trash can lids as shields and in the end, hoses used for *THE GREAT WATER FIGHT*. At one point, I looked out to see Scott leap from within the trash can, waves of water following him; he had gotten inside with a piece of hose so he could breathe, and scared the girls so badly their screams penetrated outer Alaska!

I came home from the market one day to find it had been snowing — in Southern California — and only on my house and lawn. The white substance was Christmas tree spray. The children wanted to see what our house would look like if we lived where there was snow.

We live by the water. The boys made a huge sling out of surgical tubing and took it out onto the cliff. Small water balloons could be sent a great distance; the targets were boats returning to the inside harbor. I can still remember their chatter and laughter as they told of party boats cheering them on, giving them thumbs down when the balloon missed their boat.

Five rolls of toilet paper and three trash cans of water gave birth to the Guinness-pleasing spit wad fight of the decade. It took some time for all the children involved to pick the clumps of wet paper off of every part of the yard and house. They said it was worth it.

Though some activities require "coaching" to modify behavior, creative play must not be stifled. Learning not to harm property or other people is an essential part of the process.

HANDLING NIGHTMARES

> Essential Ingredients:
> Creativity • Compassion • Communication

Remember: Nightmares are a natural phenomena of childhood.

After a full day of chasing little tots around, picking up toys, feeding, bathing and caring for them, you slip into peaceful slumber, grateful for the rest. Wha....oh, no! And you dash down the hall trying to quell the child's mind- splitting scream before the rest of the family awakens.

"I had a bad dream, Mommie." The child's voice becomes muffled as you wrap up your frightened child, rocking him/her until the tears stop.

If you've ever been on one of these nighttime adventures, you know it is useless to say, "It was just a dream, now close your eyes and go back to sleep." Soon, you will make your second dash down the hall....

Children have incredible imaginations. Why they are having a bad dream isn't important. Using their imagination to turn a negative experience into a positive one is the challenge. A friend of mine was awakened by her ten year old daughter. The child's bad dream was that she had fallen down a large pipe in the ground and couldn't get out. Her dream was precipitated by massive news coverage of a child who actually had such an experience.

The mother invited her child to use her imagination and let herself turn little like "Darby O'Gill and the Little People" (Disney). Together, a few minutes of creative imagery relieved the child's mind. Both girl and mother fell back into peaceful slumber.

The mother gets a high five for turning her parenting nightmare into a positive happening. When your peace is being disturbed, it is difficult to have the presence of mind to be compassionate **and** creative. Both are essential ingredients in assisting your child with a nightmare.

Children today are subjected to an irrational amount of information as to the harsh realities of life. Many of them understandably take their concerns with them to bed. Reading to a child before bed assists by quieting their mind.

And lastly, monitoring what your child watches on television is highly recommended. It takes time to sit down and watch a program. Your guidance is essential in this time of too much data at too early an age. Making certain programs "off limits" is a responsibility too many parents forget is theirs to take. Too much is too much!

MORE ON NIGHTMARES

> Essential Ingredients:
> Compassion • Patience • Communication

Remember: Teaching your child to handle fears is a vital aspect of learning to be inner-dependent.

I got a call one day from a mother who was hysterical because her daughter was screaming in the night and would awaken everyone in the house. The mother was a wreck from having no sleep and from worrying about the situation. The child had even been taken to a psychologist with no change in the problem. What I told her to do with her child came out of a workshop I had taken:

"Tell Katie to imagine a huge wonderful basket like an Easter basket. Have her describe the basket in great detail so she has a sense of it. Then, each night as she is going to bed, invite Katie to close her eyes, imagine her basket is by the door to her room and ask her to put all of her troubles, everything that isn't going right, her fears and her worries into the basket. She is to leave them in the basket until morning, and then she is free to pick them up again. "

Asking people to give up their fears is a major drama. By allowing the child to put fears away and pick them up again, the child is often able to put their scary thoughts aside.

Another technique that works equally well with adults as well as children is to imagine a giant balloon. Since it is your balloon, you choose the color, exact size and imagine it as vividly as you can. Now, using your imagination, put all of your worries, troubles, fears, things that didn't go well, into the balloon. See yourself letting out the string until you let go of the balloon, and watch it float away from you.

Every time a worrisome thought occurs, stop your mind and do the imagination piece with the balloon. It works!

A few children are unable to visualize. Use the word "pretend" instead of "imagine" if you see that your child has difficulty creating a picture in his/her mind.

A nightmare is a disturbing thought that penetrates the peacefulness of your mind. Using imagination, the child can learn to turn negative thoughts into positive ones — so everyone can sleep at night.

ANGER

THE RIGHT TO EXPRESS ANGER

Essential Ingredients:
Modeling • Understanding • Patience

Remember: Irritations that cannot be expressed turn into anger and eventually rage.

Anger is a feeling which must be handled differently than it has been handled in the past. I was raised, as was my generation, in a family where you did not voice or in any way express your anger. It took me a year of therapy (in my thirties) to even feel my anger let alone communicate it.

If you agree that anger needs to be expressed, you will probably be concerned as to where to draw the line in terms of limitations.

In our house, there are few rules for expressing anger:

(1) **"I" messages** instead of "you" messages must be used. (See page 76)

(2) **Talk about the problem** at hand without calling names or labeling.

(3) Take time to **cool off before you say something** that might be difficult to take back.

(4) **No physical harm** may be inflicted on anyone for any reason.

Recently, I was on a tirade and (as usual), went after Scott. Finally, he said, "You have a problem tonight and I'm not it."

Had Scott said, "You witch, you are always picking on me! You never believe I do anything right. You hate me!" I would have said, "No name calling. Talk about your feelings. Start with the word, "I". I'm listening." Name calling and accusations are subterfuge for the truth. In his original comment, Scott told the truth. His tone of voice was strong but not disrespectful. He was correct. I quickly apologized and got back on track in my own life.

"I feel really angry when I can't do what I want to do!" is a perfectly rational feeling. Wanting something is no guarantee it will happen. In the same way a pressure cooker works, expressing one's feelings of frustration releases the irritation from being controlled.

My children can express their feelings. This right has in no way diminished my authority or power in making decisions which I readily uphold. Actually, we have a much more loving, respectful, communicative relationship because feelings do not go underground.

WAYS FOR HANDLING ANGER

> Essential Ingredients:
> Modeling • Patience • Sense of Humor

Remember: Anger which is appropriately vented is less likely to turn into violence, psychosomatic illness or depression.

Problem: Two children are in a heated fist fight. Separate the two, then use the following dialogue. "Jeff I know you are really angry, but Brian is going to tell me what's on his mind and no matter what he says, you are going to be quiet. You will have your turn, but for now you are to stand there and you do not do or say anything. Understand?"

So Brian, being really angry, will have quite a bit to say. Let him talk until he literally runs out of talk. Then give Brian the same instructions — to stand there and be quiet — until Jeff is finished.

Go back and forth from one boy (or girl) to the next. Both children will run out of steam and will probably walk off together to play once again. I call this "The Cote Method" after a teacher/friend who taught it to me.

We have a punching bag in our garage. Venting anger is the purpose of having the bag there, and I encourage all of us to use it.

Those plastic creatures with sand in their base are great for little kids to vent their anger as they fall down but bounce back.

Running is a great way to move anger through your body. Having two children who are fighting run down opposite sides of the street and back can regain their perspective so they can talk.

Once when Scott was small, I gave him a piece of paper and some crayons saying, "Draw a picture about your feelings." Later, his picture showed one person in the middle of the page, with airplanes dropping bombs, tanks shooting, and soldiers shooting at that person. "Is that me?" I asked and he replied, "Uh-huh!" "Boy, you're really mad at me, aren't you?" I said with no trace of shock. He began, "Yea, I got you good! (pause) It's just pretend cuz I'm mad." Having vented his anger, Scott and I could talk about the problem and begin to build a bridge between the two of us. Both Scott and I have a temper. We work very hard to express our feelings in appropriate ways, and don't let anger build up inside of us for long periods of time.

Anger appropriately expressed promotes emotional health.

TEACH APPROPRIATE WAYS OF RELEASING ANGER

Essential Ingredients:
Modeling • Patience • Understanding

Remember: Your children will become mirrors as to how you handle your anger.

All of us have let little things pile up only to become a raging, spewing volcano over something of very small consequence. It simply isn't fair to take out all of your anger on your own family. Children soon learn to discount the feelings of a parent who rants and raves instead of communicating his/her feelings and wants.

Breaking a habit is not easy. See if you can make a game out of changing your pattern if you tend to scream at your children a lot. For one day, make a personal rule that you cannot yell at your children. When the urge to scream comes, stop! Go immediately to the ice box and carry an ice cube around until you "cool off." Sounds silly? That's the point. Doing something silly gets your attention. Then you can make a conscious decision to change how you talk to your children.

Nearly all of what you teach about anger will be through modeling. If you do not allow any dissension whatsoever in your home, your family will learn to put their anger under-ground. The main problem with this plan is that everyone must find a safe place to handle that feeling. If you treat even minor infractions with rage, and especially with physical assault, your children may become volatile or totally withdrawn. The emotional damage which results from physical abuse is very difficult to erase.

Anger left untapped may turn to resentment and if left to fester even more to revenge. Our society is the bi-product of anger turned to revenge. It is essential we teach our children that anger itself is a natural feeling and that inappropriate behavior following anger is the problem for which a solution is sought.

Teaching your children to express their anger without being disrespectful is difficult. The boundary lines are not well-defined. My rules are: Use an "I" message, No name calling and No physical abuse. My teenagers and I rarely get into shouting fights any more because we have learned to talk things out before something small gets blown out of proportion.

I have much more value for the respect that results from two people telling each other the truth, than I do the "Yes, Ma'm" variety which looks respectful.

HANDLING SIBLING ANGER

> Essential Ingredients:
> Patience • Understanding • Trust

Remember: If you handle all the battles your child gets into for him/her, that child will not learn self care.

Teasing is probably the most common cause for sibling fights. Often, it seems as if one child read a book on special ways to torment and rile the others — and your life becomes that of a fragmented referee.

Teasing has a purpose. The bottom-line purpose is to involve the parent in their fight. Another reason can be to express resentment or anger. Whatever the reason, your children have a right to fight. You have the right to determine **how** they fight.

In our home, fighting is allowed as long as these rules are followed: (1) No hitting is allowed by children or adults (2) You may not continually infringe upon the peace of the rest of the family with your fight (3) Use your words ("I" messages, no name calling, talk about the problem).

If your children get into a yelling fight at the dinner table they need to stop it or take the fight somewhere else. A child who hits another child receives some sort of consequence for that action. (Go sit in the dining room for ten minutes). Hitting is not allowed. If both children hit each other, have no sympathy for wounds. "I am sorry you are hurt. When you learn to use your words instead of your fists there won't be any hurts," is all you need to say. Both children receive a consequence for their choice.

When two children constantly fight (the dynamic is that one teases, one hits), you need to stop this behavior. Don't get involved in endless explanations, "You two obviously can't get along today, so you are not to be in the same room at the same time until dinner. This includes the television room. Work with the children at another time on "using their words instead of fighting". Getting along is a choice each of us make. Some children need more assistance in this area.

In a society that watches endless hours of TV where people beat each other senseless, it is difficult to teach non-violence. This teaching must start young and be enforced by every member of the family. Parents who use words to teach and give logical consequences for inappropriate behavior find that hitting their children becomes unnecessary. (My way of handling anger may not be your way.) Think about how you handle anger in your family and do what works for you.

ALTERNATIVES TO ANGER IN
CORRECTING PHONE ETIQUETTE

> Essential Ingredients:
> Awareness • Self-correction • Being Inept

Remember: Parents do not do everything perfectly. Mistakes are a natural part of learning.

Rather than getting angry when something is done inappropriately (which is to say not the way you want it done), have a talk about alternatives.

If your child is inept at answering the phone say, "I have a concern about how you just answered the phone. It is important to me that messages from this home are friendly. If you choose to pick up the phone, please use your friendly voice in the future, OK?"

If your boy and girl hate it when one is mistaken for the other, suggest, "If you answer the phone with 'This is Kathleen, hello!' or 'Hello, Kathleen speaking,' no one will mistake you for him. What else could you say that wouldn't feel silly or stupid?"

When two or more children make a B-line for a ringing phone only to engage in a major battle over who is going to answer it, try this: Have each child pick a favorite color and make a circle or square in each child's color. The color for one child is put on each of the phones (every day or every week). That child has first option for answering the telephone when it rings.

When a child forgets (let's say it is the blue child's turn to get the phone and the yellow child gets it anyway), the excuse given is "Well, I just wanted to do it!" Put your anger aside. Wanting something when you want it is a common trait for all children. To the "yellow child" you say, "I know you really want to answer the phone and it is (Sue's) turn today. Your turn will be another day. If the phone rings again today, you need to let (Sue) get it — even if that is a hard thing to do." If the "yellow child" is persistent (remember, persistence is a quality to preserve along with self-discipline), intercept the child on the way to the phone if possible and give the same (unemotional) message as before. If you aren't able to intercept the child, give a consequence for that child's choice (sit in the dining room for ten minutes). At the end of the consequence, ask that child about the rule for answering the phone. Once a child believes you will stick-to-your-guns, such reinforcement will become unnecessary.

WRITING A LETTER TO REROUTE ANGER

> Essential Ingredients:
> Modeling • Time • Trusting Yourself

Remember: Teaching children to channel their anger may be a very large contributor towards each of them being loving human beings.

Many researchers and psychologists have said a person who is truly able to give and receive love is someone who owns and works effectively with their anger.

A helpful tool for both of my children has been to write an angry letter. You simply sit down with a piece of paper and write the person for whom you hold the anger every single thing you would say if you could say anything.

Some children, having difficulty approaching anger itself, might begin with other feelings: hurt, afraid, disappointed, helpless, or upset.

The only rule for this process is to tear up the letter and throw it away after writing it. The purpose is to re-channel your energy, not trash another person in a non-personal way. This is not a substitute for talking about your feelings but a way of calming down so you can talk.

Some children have a temper, some do not. Whether your child has a long or a short fuse, from nine years old up, writing an angry letter can be a very useful tool.

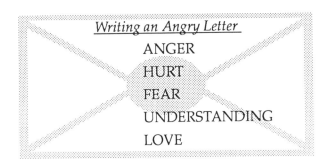

Writing an Angry Letter
ANGER
HURT
FEAR
UNDERSTANDING
LOVE

MORE WORD WATCHING

> Essential Ingredients:
> Listen to Yourself • Think it Through • Mistakes are OK

Remember: Making children responsible for <u>your</u> feelings instills resentment and teaches dependency.

A common phrase used in parenting is, "You make me..." **Nobody makes anybody feel anything.** Wait a minute you say, what about anger? You are driving on the freeway and someone cuts you off. You jam on the breaks and talk to your heart trying to calm it down. One time someone cuts you off, you say, "Oops!" and stay calm. Another time, you yell, scream and give hand gestures. What changed? You **chose** to get angry one of the two times.

"I feel angry when you yell in the car" states the feeling and the problem. "You make me so angry!" gives your children the power of controlling your feelings. More important, such a statement does not give any information about the problem. It is important to say what you want done along with stating your feelings: "I feel angry when you yell in the car and I want you to stop yelling right now, please."

Even if a child runs into you and you spill the juice, use words that correct the problem. Say, "Oops! The juice is spilled. Please get a towel and help me clean it off the floor." As you are cleaning up the spilled juice, say to your child, "You need to watch where you are going next time."

When a child comes in after dark, you might say, "Where have you been? You made me sick to my stomach, I was so worried." To get off of the "you made me" words and teach with understanding, say instead, "I'm glad you are home. I was worried that something had happened to you. The later it got, the more worried I felt. Tell me what happened that you are so late." Once I tiraded Kathleen for being late and scaring me to death only to be told that a car had hit a cat and she chose to stay with the cat until someone came to assist.

The words "you made me" take power away from the parent and disempower the child. I recommend erasing those three words from words you choose to use.

TEENAGERS

STICK UP FOR THE THINGS IN WHICH YOU BELIEVE

> Essential Ingredients
> Tenacity • Communication • Patience

Remember: Do not compromise on your personal integrity or anything which is really important to you.

The best advice I received in my training for parenting teens came from Dorothy Corkille Briggs. She explained that a teenager's homework is to break away from the parent and to begin making decisions for him/herself. In deciding how to parent your teenagers, Dorothy had one rule: Decide which of your rules you would die for and let the rest go.

When I was in high school, one of my best friends was killed by a drunk driver. I have no sense of humor whatsoever about driving and drinking. Both of my children are aware that if they ever drink and drive they will lose their car and suffer from irrational consequences.

I do not support drinking alcohol. The rule about drinking is separate from the rule about drinking and driving. What I want my children to understand is that if either one chooses to break the rule about drinking, he/she had best think twice about driving and drinking. Any time of the night, I will go and get one of them if they have chosen to drink. I will not be at the jail to bail them out if they choose to drink and drive.

These are the rules for which I would die:

- *My word is law — when I ask that something is done it needs to be done.*

- *Helping to keep the house in order is a requirement of living in our home.*

- *Harming property or other people is never acceptable.*

- *No one needs your judgment — don't judge others.*

- *Supporting each other and treating each other w/ respect in the good and the bad times is an essential ingredient of being a family.*

- *Tell the truth at all times.*

- *Stealing (even in the smallest sense) is not allowed.*

- *Love God, love yourself and love each other. Until all of us live by these three simple Commandments, the world will not know peace.*

GETTING OUT OF DIFFICULT SITUATIONS

> Essential Ingredients:
> Communication • Agreements • Sense of Humor

Remember: Peer pressure is a huge item to take into consideration when expecting your teen to rescue him/herself from a tricky situation.

It is very difficult for your teenager to break away from an undesirable group activity. The stress in this situation increases significantly if your teen is dependent on someone in the group for a ride home.

I have an agreement with my teenagers that they may call me any time night or day and I will retrieve them without any questions. I also keep money in a jug from which they could pay a cab driver if I were not at home.

Getting into a teenage event that escalates to the point of "feeling uncomfortable" is not unusual. Too many teens go with the crowd because there doesn't seem to be another option.

I can understand being in a situation that suddenly gets "uncomfortable." I do not condone staying in that situation using the excuse of "there was nothing I could do." Not true! "Because everybody else was doing it" has never been an acceptable excuse for me. My standard response is, "Great, and if everyone suddenly ran off a cliff would you join them?" Because I understand the depth of peer pressure, it is my job to provide an alternate choice.

I also give both teenagers carte blanch permission to use me as an excuse not to go somewhere or do something. "My mother will kill me," or "I told my mom I would be home by twelve and she'll have a shotgun waiting if I don't," or to call and use a password (Mommie Dearest) to indicate that, even though there is to be arguing on his/her side, I am to say no to the request at hand.

S: "Hello, Mommie Dearest, Todd wants to know if I can spend the night."

M: "You want me to say no, so the answer is no, Scott."

S: "Come on, Mom, give me a break!"

M: "Tell him you welshed on cleaning your room and are grounded tonight."

S: "Mom, I'll clean my room tomorrow. Please, Mommie Dearest."

M: "Drop in a crack, Jack. By the way, now that I've mentioned your room...."

S: "Ok....(dejectedly) I'll be home in a half an hour."

DO NOT USE NICKNAMES

> Essential Ingredients:
> Alertness • Awareness • Sense of Humor

Remember: Looking cool is the teen's game. A cute nickname may become a weapon used against your precious child.

When Kathleen was little, we nicknamed her "Muffin" because she was crinkly and smelled good. Later, her special name got changed to "Muff".

Scott, who was a whopping eleven pounds at birth (Breathe! I had him Cesarean!), was initially called "Shamu" but soon became dubbed as, "Baby Ducks".

For years, I called both children alternately by their given names and their nicknames. Then, without notice, I was expected to drop the nicknames.

Starting to talk to Kathleen in front of her friends I would begin with, "Muff..." The stern admonishment, "Mo-om!" would bring me to my senses. Naturally all the teens (who were gathered for an ancient ritual called, "What shall we do tonight?" For which the password is, "I don't know.") snickered and mimicked me by calling Muff...er..Kathleen... "Muff."

Scott grew by leaps and bounds from his non-humble beginning. I still laugh remembering the whiplash turn of his head and instantaneous "Don't you dare!" stare when he was on the high school basketball team and I started to yell, "Hang in there, Baa...")!

There's a point I need to continually make in writing this book: JUST WHEN YOU THINK YOU'VE FIGURED OUT SOME PATTERN OR REASON FOR RESPONSE, HE/SHE WILL CHANGE. Note...

Kathleen has a friend who puts an "Mc" on the front of every name (I am "McMom"). Recently, I heard Lisa call Kathleen "McMuff", so I apologized to Kathleen as it seemed obvious, "it was my fault that Lisa knew that name, and I'm trying to break my bad habits, and I'm really sorry and..." And it was Kathleen's idea.

Somewhere in the younger years, I would say to Scott as he was leaving for school, "Bye Baby Ducks" and he'd respond, "Bye Mommagoose!" Recently, he and his other six foot plus boy friends were leaving and he turned saying, "Later, Goose!" so I laughed and responded, "Take care, Ducks!" I heard his friends ask, "Goose! Ducks?" to which he responded, "Nicknames." The choice to use nicknames is a personal one.

GIVING COMPLIMENTS TO TEENAGERS

> Essential Ingredients:
> Communication • Perseverance • Kindness

Remember: Just because your teenager doesn't gurgle and snuggle up to you when you give a compliment doesn't mean compliments aren't needed.

Teenagers have a self-defense mechanism which does not always include accepting compliments. I've read that over 80% of teens do not like the way they look. In addition, the Gallup Poll tells us that 4 out of 5 people have low self- esteem. Low self-esteemers cannot take in compliments.

If you say to your teenager one morning, "You look beautiful today!" the teen's response might be, "What? Don't you see this glob of hair sticking out here, and my left eye is red, and...." Suddenly, your intent to give encouragement turned into a massive self-destructive monologue. Nothing you can say thereafter will penetrate the teen's gloom.

To begin with, "you" messages don't work. "You" has to do with your BEING. In giving compliments "You" is too general. See if you can feel the difference between these "you" and "I" messages.

No: "You look nice, today."
Yes: "I like that shirt with those pants."

No: "You are always so thoughtful."
Yes: "My heart felt happy when I saw the flowers in my room."

No: "You did a good job."
Yes: "The kitchen never looked cleaner, thanks!"

No: "You are such a good person!"
Yes: "I value kindness wherever I find it; I noticed you helped your grandmother carry her things to the car."

No: "You are always so thoughtful!"
Yes: "Thanks for helping your sister pick up that mess."

Note: "You" messages are often general. Telling someone he/she is"always so thoughtful" could set off a lot of negative self-talk if that statement isn't totally true. Use the words "always" and "never" judicially.

"I" messages usually start with the word "I" and are to be followed with a specific remark about what happened. It is not easy to personalize every message, and the time you invest in this procedure will bring immeasurable returns. (See page 76 for more information on "I" messages.)

TEENAGERS WITH OPTIONS MAKE BETTER CHOICES!

> Essential Ingredients:
> Trust • Communication • Flexibility

Remember: There comes a time when you need to give in on some rules and die for the others.

Because I get up in the morning at six o'clock, it is difficult for me to stay awake past eleven o'clock at night. Teenagers are night-owls. Even if they are at home, they like to stay up until unholy hours and then sleep all morning, if possible.

At some point, I taught myself to go to bed and sleep , often before my teenagers did. For years, I've asked my teens to let me know they are in for the night by awakening me.

When Kathleen turned eighteen I asked her what she wanted from me in terms of rule changes or attitudes. (It is best, I have found, to ask rather than discover a want through rebellion or other hostilities.) She asked if she could not have a curfew on weekends. Also, she wanted to forgo the rule to awaken me — it scared her to startle me!

My basic desire to control my children was definitely jiggled by both requests. As I've told both Kathleen and Scott, "Get in touch with the fact that I want you in bed at nine o'clock with your teddy bears, safe and sound, and anything else is pushin' it — so you need to work with me on anything different."

We decided to have a trial period of one month. I think she stayed out until four o'clock one time, and then seemed to come in earlier than she had before we made our agreement. Kathleen has proven herself to be responsible since she was little, so this gesture of trust was easier to give than I imagined.

The second request was more difficult because it was un-nerving to awaken, listen and not know if everyone was home. The plan we devised is in effect today: When I go to bed, I turn on the hall light. The last teen in (they can tell by how many cars are in the garage) turns off that light. If I awaken and the hall light is off, I know my chicks are in bed — with their teddy bears.

Decisions about trust and giving responsibility need to be made according to the past record of the individual child. The goal, once again, is to teach your child to be inner-dependent. Giving a child your trust is an absolutely vital link in an endless chain of building high self-esteem.

TEACHING FOGGING

Essential Ingredients:
Patience • Understanding • Communication

Remember: Your teenagers will deal with a great deal of judgment and verbal abuse.

The harsh reality of a teenagers life is staggering. Teens are subjected to a huge amount of verbal abuse. They treat each other terribly. Put-downs seems to be a form of humor which has become acceptable to our youth. Spotlighting differences is the focus of their verbal tongue lashings. The harm that is done, individually, is immeasurable.

Fogging is an assertive training technique taught to me by Manuel J. Smith **(When I Say No I Feel Guilty)**. It is to be used when you do not want to educate or engage in verbal combat with the assault person.

When you throw a rock in a fog bank, it does not get hurt. It does not throw the rock back. The fog takes the rock into itself and is not damaged by the process.

When you "fog" someone, you simply agree with the possibility of what is being said:

A: "You are a nerd."
B: "You could think that. "(fogging)

A: "I do think that. You never do anything right!"
B: "sometimes that's true." (fogging)

A: "You'll never be a winner."
B: "That might be true." (fogging)

Saying "You could be right" doesn't mean you agree, it simply means you won't engage in an argument.

If what someone says **is** true (You said you'd return my record and you haven't), the possible response is, "That's true." If what is said is not true, ("You're a nerd"), one choice for a response is, "That's possible."

<u>Phrases to express your indifference include:</u>

> *You may be right.*
> *You could think that.*
> *That's possible.*
> *You could be right.*
> *I can see how you would think that.*

Will your teenager use this technique on you? If you are the authority, no. It's a vital skill for them to know in order to protect themselves against the pressures of life.

THE BROKEN RECORD

> Essential Ingredients:
> Perseverance • Sense of Humor • Patience

Remember: It is not enough to tell your children to follow your morals and values — you must teach them how.

I am indebted to all I've learned from writing Project Self-Esteem in terms of this vital skill, both for parents themselves, and for their children.

When a record is exposed to extreme temperatures, it often plays the same thing over and over. The Broken Record is a way of holding your place by repeating chosen words, and allows you to be kind in the process.

The **Broken Record** has a **KIND STATEMENT** and a **POLICY STATEMENT** as its basic elements. The **kind statement** lets the listener feel you have empathy for them, and the **policy statement** is the place you hold your ground.

A: "Hey, that sweater is great! Can I borrow it, tomorrow?"
B: "I'm glad you like my sweater (kind statement) and I never loan my clothes." (policy statement)
A: "Cool, man but I'm your pal."
B: "You are my pal (kind statement) and I never loan my clothes (policy statement)."

Question: What if you do loan clothes, but don't want to loan your sweater to this person?
B: "I'm glad you like my sweater (kind) and I don't feel comfortable loaning it to you." (policy)
A: "What's this comfortable stuff? I'm your pal!"
B: "I'm glad we're pals (kind) and I don't feel comfortable loaning you this sweater." (policy)
A: "Well, I guess we aren't friends after all."
B: "I hope whether we are friends or not doesn't depend upon loaning a sweater, (kind) and I don't feel comfortable loaning you this sweater."

A: (To a teenager entering a party)"Here, have a beer!"
B: "Thanks for the offer, I don't want a drink right now"
A: "Come on, man...chill out...and relax...here!"
B: "Thanks, but I don't want a beer right now."
A: "Are you some kind of goody-goody?"
B: "I plan to chill out and relax and I don't want a drink right now."

Research indicates that 12% of teens can say they don't drink as the reason to turn someone down. The rest of the teens need a tool that assists in putting off the person who is being insistent.

PARENT'S USE OF THE BROKEN RECORD

> Essential Ingredients:
> Perseverance • Patience • Practice

Remember: The "whittle, whittle, whittle game" gets to be very tiring. The broken record is a vital tool for parents.

First use a kind statement and then use a policy statement to talk to your children about the following:

A: Mom, can I go to the rock concert in San Francisco this weekend.

B: (Inside, you scream, "What?" Then you remember the broken record.) I'm sorry, that doesn't feel like a safe thing to do, so, no, you cannot go."

A: But Mom, all my friends are going.

B: It will be difficult to be the only one not going (kind statement) and that doesn't feel like a safe thing to do, so, no you cannot go. (policy statement)

A: Mom, I promise I won't do anything stupid or use drugs or get in any trouble. Please!

B: I trust you to make reasonable choices (kind statement) and it doesn't feel like a safe thing to do, so, you cannot go. (policy statement)

A: You treat me like a baby. All of my friends' parents trust their kids.

B: I realize saying no looks like distrust (kind statement) but it doesn't feel safe for you to go, so, my answer is no. (policy statement)

Notice the second part of that dialogue is repetitive while the first part changes to encompass compassion for the teen's feelings. Once you begin to use this tool, your teen will recognize the broken record in use and will quickly give in to your choice.

A: "Scott I want you to pick up your room before your grandparents arrive for dinner."

B: "Grandma doesn't care about my room being messy, she loves me for me."

A: "I love you for you too, and I want your room picked up before they arrive for dinner."

B: "That's not enough time to pick up that mess!"

A: "Nevertheless, I want you to pick up your room before your grandparents arrive."

The broken record may be used when someone wants you to do something you don't want to do, when you are accused of something you didn't do, or at any time you want to hold your line.

CURFEW, DITCHING SCHOOL AND "BAD" BEHAVIOR

> Essential Ingredients:
> Patience • Communication • Follow-through

Remember: These emotional, irrational, illogical teenage humans are making a stand towards independence. If you have done your job well, they will break away.

One of my favorite Erma Bombeck writings has to do with laboring over making a kite, carefully letting it out a little at a time, and finally, letting it go. The part in the middle — the letting out the string — is one of the most difficult times for most parents. Questions fill your mind: Did I teach them enough? Will he/she be safe out there? Can he/she endure the pain of this time? Is it really time?

The following suggestions can assist you with your very individual job of guiding and at the same time, letting go of your teenager:

1. CURFEW: I checked around to see what other teen curfews were, and then made my own decision. Generally speaking, the week-day curfew changed from not going out on a school night to nine-then-ten o'clock. Week-end curfew began at eleven o'clock and eventually moved to one o'clock. Our rule is simple: Break the rule and I change the rule. If you are to be in at midnight, twelve-fifteen is only acceptable once. Then the curfew is changed to eleven o'clock for one week.

    "In by twelve or phone by eleven" is my request. Sometimes, a reasonable request to extend the time is granted. I ask them to phone me before the curfew deadline as worrying is not good for my heart.

2. DITCHING SCHOOL: If the school calls to ask if your teen is home ill and you have no idea where he/she is, it is best to tell the truth and let your teen have his/her consequences. Ditching school a couple of times is probably worth the consequence to a teenager trying his/her wings, but repetitive infringement of that rule needs to be quelled. I know a woman who, for two weeks, went to school with her teenage son who had been repeatedly ditching school. She sat outside the classroom, walked to her son's class with him, and took him home after school. Was he embarrassed? Yes. Did he every ditch again? No.

3. "BAD" BEHAVIOR: The difference between frisky and "bad" behavior is important to determine. One is to be allowed, the other is to be stopped. Consequences tend to stop frisky behavior from escalating.

BABYSITTING, GETTING A JOB, AND EMOTIONS

> **Essential Ingredients:**
> Communication • Perseverance • Patience

1. BABYSITTING: A great way to earn money is to baby-sit. My Kathleen wrote to the Library of Congress for their guidelines on babysitting. She had her check-off list at hand whenever she booked a babysitting job. What I remember is she left me the phone number where she would be. She required that the child's parents leave a number where they could be reached and the number of a neighbor in case there was an emergency. She also requested phone numbers for a possible emergency. The parents were told that she didn't like to be told her job was from seven to midnight and have them drift in at one o'clock. If they were going to be later than midnight, she would appreciate a call. If a couple didn't come home in the vicinity of the time they said, Kathleen would not baby-sit for them again.

    The main thing to impress on your children is what an incredible responsibility it is to baby-sit, and that their focus needs to be on the children at all times.

2. GETTING A JOB: Kathleen began working at sixteen. She wanted to have her own car and her own spending money. Her grades were high, so she could handle working and going to school. Scott, being in sports, and needing to focus on school, has not had a steady job to date (he is 17). It seems as if there is no time for our children to be young any more. Life has many financial requirements and there is so little one can do that doesn't cost money. I think the key is balance. Can your child balance his/her life with a job and school? If the answer is no, something else needs to happen. Communication, as always, is the key to working out the best plan for each child.

3. EMOTIONS: Boys store emotions because it isn't macho to be emotional. So a teenage boy's energy can be very loud, aggressive and rowdy. Teen boys fill the room with the odor of stale sweat socks and a certain volume which defies being ignored. They laugh at anything even slightly resembling crudeness and seem to have a fixation on anything suggestive of the word penis. Put downs are king, and I have seldom heard of teenage boys sitting around discussing their feelings — or even mentioning that they have any.

    Teenage girls can be a cyclone of emotion. Something as innocuous as, "Hello Sweetheart!" can set off tears and a fit of expression far greater than the situation/problem. Teenage girls talk about little else but feelings — and much of that talk is done on the phone.

TONE OF VOICE AND BORROWING THE CAR

> **Essential Ingredients:**
> Communication • Perseverance • Kindness

Remember: Teens need coaches not wardens.

1. TONE OF VOICE: It seems that a requirement of turning into a teenager is to try out a snooty tone of voice with one or more parent. The general message given is that some low-life adult is meddling into a private realm. Breaking away or not, I cannot handle a snippy, stupid-idiot tone of voice. When one of my teens snips, I calmly say, "You know, I would really like to hear what it is you have to say. But I have the funniest ears — they can't listen to that tone of voice. How about saying what you have to say in a way that I can hear?" Teenagers are very economical — they hate repetitive lectures. About the third time you begin your little spiel, you will hear, "Sorry, (in a lilt designed in heaven) hello, Mom!"

2. BORROWING THE FAMILY CAR(S): One summer morning, I walked into the garage, thinking I was going to go do errands. No car! Oops! I had forgotten Scott had taken it that day. From their sixteenth birthday on, a teenager has one thought: How can I get the car today, tonight, tomorrow, next week, next year....

    Then, when you finally have "your turn" with your own car, left behind are stale french fries, smelly sweat socks and there is no gas in the gas tank.

    In our family, we make agreements about use of the family car. If you use gas, you are to put gas back into the tank before the next person needs the car. If you are going to be later than your agreement, you need to phone. Keeping the car clean on the inside and outside is the job of the teenager who has the right to use the car. Not done? Sorry, no use of car.

    Any tickets (parking or otherwise) are paid for by the offender, and any raise in insurance belongs to the offender as well.

    There is something wonderful and scary about having teenagers who can take themselves wherever they want to go. The freedom is wonderful — not having a car to use whenever you want it is less wonderful. In the end, it all works out. If you have taught your teenager to respect the law, their safety margin expands. **Whatever you do, make stringent rules and enforce them against drinking and driving. Be sure you model following this rule as well.**

WHEN TEENS WHO ARE AWAY DON'T WRITE

> Essential Ingredients:
> Time • Walk in Their Moccasins • Humor

Remember: Children who are away may not write because they don't want you to know they are homesick.

My father invented a form of communication which we called, **"MAILMEBACKOGRAMS"**. It is a guaranteed way of hearing from your child when he/she is away, and lends itself to a rare form of expression, especially humor. To illustrate, here are a few lines, written to Scott when he was at Wilderness Survival Camp in Wyoming (we live in California).

Please check one or more answers or add your own comment and return to me in the next mail:

Dear ☐ Super-cook ☐ Best Family in the West ☐_____

I'd write you more often but
    ☐ they won't let us off of our ball and chains
    ☐ they make us write with blood — our own
    ☐ no news is good news
    ☐ _____

We went on our four day survival outing and
    ☐ we survived
    ☐ we starved
    ☐ it was a toss up between hungry and scared
    ☐ your cooking is really looking good
    ☐ _____

In closing, I will fill in the blanks
  Living in the open space is_____
  The food here is_____
  The hardest thing each day is_____
  The best thing about each day is_____

Please send ☐ Food ☐ Money ☐ Food and Money ☐_____

A "MAILMEBACK-O-GRAM" can be written by one family member or by every family member. Kathleen and I made up things to put into them, laughing and imagining what Scott would say. Then, when the "gram" was returned, we all laughed at Scott's answers. We put the "MAILMEBACKOGRAMS" into photo albums where treasured memories are stored.

LETTING GO

> Essential Ingredients:
> Communication • Feel Your Feelings • Trust

Remember: That your teen is emotionally breaking away is not a comment against you — it is their homework.

Somewhere within the scope of the time called "the teens" the no longer small child for which you trained yourself to continually watch, emotionally moves away from you. Even when you understand that dynamic and its necessity, there can be pain with this sudden realization of "no more babies".

From my journal: *"My once chatty, bubbling Kathleen with lots of time to share the day's adventures has turned within. Though friendly, she is withdrawn. My mind says it is time for her to pull away, and my heart is filled with tears.*

"Oh, beautiful butterfly, must you go so soon? I have lots of other ideas to share, lots of chitty chat left over. How will I let this time be? How will I let go and let you make your own way? Tears roll down my face as my mind searches for reasons to stall for more time — and I quietly raise my hand, opening it, to release my butterfly."

Then, before I knew it, I was writing in my journal again: *"Down the stairs, out the door — three guys, two chicks. Talking, they walk away. As I watch, my mind asks, 'Is it time...already?' My friend laughs at me, but he has not walked all the way from baby to this six foot four adolescent. 'Is it time?' isn't a complaint — just an acknowledgment that my last child is no longer a child. Change...it's all a mother knows."*

And, if you have done your job right, the breaking away however difficult, will not be awash in conflict and hurtful dialogue. When your teen successfully breaks away and the friendship remains, you need ask yourself no questions about the quality of job you did.

When your last child breaks away, it is now your job to bring something meaningful into your life to fill the void. I have seen too many women wither away when their teens left. Both men and women need to commit themselves to new challenges. Get involved in something that contributes to the world being a better place. (Present Project Self-Esteem in your local school.) Remember all those times you asked for one minute to yourself? Well, now you have them! Even for those who make it look easy, letting go is seldom if ever an easy process.

DIVORCE

TELLING YOUR CHILDREN

> Essential Ingredients:
> Truth • Compassion • Kindness

Remember: The grown ups are getting a divorce. No matter what you say the children feel as if they are being divorced as well.

Even if a child has watched the relationship of the parents deteriorate, the news of divorce is received with fear. The child wants to know what is going to happen to him or her.

However rational the cause, the child feels really angry with the mother, father and him/herself. ALL CHILDREN BELIEVE THEY ARE IN SOME WAY THE CAUSE FOR THE DIVORCE. Therefore, the child also feels guilty. Even if the home environment has been horrible, the child prefers it to change, and so the child feels intense fear along with sadness.

Whether it is best for both parents or one parent to talk to the children depends upon the individuals involved. It is important that both parties take responsibility for the decision and don't begin the process of change by blaming each other. Even if one adult is the cause of the separation, the child does not need that information because it forces him/her to choose between parents in terms of allegiance.

"Your father and I have tried to work out our problems and we cannot. We are getting a divorce. We want you to know we both love you and you will not have to choose which one of us you love most. You will live with me, but you can see your Dad any time you want. I want to talk to you more about this, but for now, it seems enough to feel your feelings. If you would like to punch the punching bag, cry or scream, I think it would help. I'm sorry you need to go through this.Do you want to say anything right now?"

Even if the child knows it is coming, he/she can't take in much more information than the word "divorce." If the child cries, holding him/her is very appropriate. If the child asks you to leave the room, do it. Each person in a divorce must handle the reality of what's happening individually. You can assist, but you cannot protect your children from their pain. If you try to save them from their pain they will not build enough emotional muscle to endure all the changes that lie ahead, especially within the structure of safety they called home.

DIFFICULT CHANGES FOR CHILDREN

Essential Ingredients
Trust • Communication • Listening

Remember: You do not need to create an unreal reality to protect your children.

Some couples, in an attempt to spare their children, go overboard to paint a picture of "sainthood" for each other. A parent is a human being with positive and negative qualities. It is very difficult for children to be given a picture of perfection about one adult only to discover the truth of their imperfection.

It is equally difficult for a child to dissect your anger from the truth of any information about the other adult. If you "trash" the other parent verbally, it confuses your children. They think they have to take sides. Sometimes, when children see the mother's hurt (assuming the children live with her), they take her side. Taking sides splits a child's heart.

If your ex-spouse is a (blank-blank), the children will figure it out in time. Their picture may not be the same as yours in the long run. It is the right of every child to have their own relationship with each parent.

When either parent dates it is traumatic for the child. The irrational belief that something will happen to bring the two of you back together is shattered. Expecting your children to be nice to the intruder in their dream is asking a lot. Saying you want to have some adult fun is all you need to say about dating. Being lonely, needing support, etc. are all emotions the child can't fathom — nor should they be asked to add to the burden or their own needs, your needs as well.

If the children live with the mother, the father immediately becomes the "good guy." He picks them up, plays with them, takes them special places and doesn't have to deal with the day-to-day hardships of living together. It is easy for the woman to resent this role. Facts are, it exists. The best you can do for yourself and the children is to accept your role and stick to your guns in terms of creating some structure for the safety and well-being of your children. Your ex-husband may never get what you went through to give them this foundation, but you will.

Fathers need to be careful not to undermine the mother's authority or to say negative things about her to the children. Your children are not your dumping ground. They are small humans who are trying to help both grown ups through something they cannot understand.

DIFFICULT CHANGES FOR CHILDREN #2

> Essential Ingredients:
> Communication • Respect • Trust

Remember: Your children have the right to learn their own lessons from change.

Divorce is a very painful, lonely experience for the adults involved. In order to cope with such pain, it is easy to turn your children into your buddies. Telling your children the details of your money worries, dating problems, troubles with their father, etc. places an unnecessary burden on them. They are children, not adults — and they are not your best friends in the sense of sharing everything.

It is reasonable to ask children to assist more with the care of the house after a divorce. It is not reasonable to turn the mothering job over to them — even if you work. Assisting and taking responsibility for something are two different things. Taking more responsibility is positive, taking *the* responsibility is harmful.

It is incomprehensibly difficult to go through your own pain, take charge of the money earning, keep the house in order and deal with the pain of your children. And those are the job requirements when your children live with you. Be willing to let some things go: The house may not be as clean as it was for awhile. Dinners may be mostly hot dogs and Spagetti-o's. Compromise on perfection; it's a matter of survival.

By the way, as the mother in a divorce, it is equally easy to want to baby your children You feel guilty for putting them through this drama, and so "smother mother" can come forth. If you catch yourself doing "Super-Mom," stop! If you baby your children and let them get away with murder, stop! If you watch them like a hawk trying to protect them from even invisible problems, stop! Try to watch yourself with your children (as if you are seeing yourself on a video). If you don't like the picture, change your script.

Some parents don't visit the children. If the other parent lives in another town, that fact is easier to accept, but if the parent doesn't come around because he/she doesn't want to deal with his/her hurt, the children may get hurt and feel resentful. You can't change someone else. Working out a way to accept the truth and handle your feelings is the only job you have in such a situation. You are not a wizard. Do not interpret why he/she does what he/she does. Invite your children to call and ask him/her. If that is impossible, simply say you don't know. It is hurtful to be abandoned. It is more hurtful to be fed lies about what's happening only to have to face the truth later.

LETTING YOUR CHILDREN HANDLE THEIR OWN PAIN

> Essential Ingredients:
> Trust • Patience • Understanding

Remember: Divorce is a reality in your child's life. How you treat your child gives a message about his/her own capability of handling problems.

It was in July that Dick and I told our children we were getting a divorce. The night before I told them, I sat weeping in the corner of the couch, all night long. It was one of the most difficult things I have ever done, and the memory of each child's response forever lingers in my mind. Kathleen knew it was coming. She wept as I rocked her.

Scott had never seen Dick or me fight, so he thought I was kidding. I assured him I was not kidding. He swung around, put his feet on the wall (he was nine), tears rolling out of his eyes, and said, "Please leave my room!"

Kathleen retreated into herself. Scott had never given anyone any trouble. He had been a lovable, bouncing ball of energy with a stable disposition bordering on hilarity. He became an angry, defiant, irritable person who was a walking fight looking for a place to land. Scott constantly got into trouble at school (a first), and I would put him to bed at night exhausted from the endless combat. Over and over, I repeated these words: "I know you want this to be different than it is, but this is what is happening. I know you have it inside of you some place to handle your pain. I will help you find that place. I will not be the dumping ground for your anger."

I remember Kathleen asking me how I could stand it. I replied, "If I thought this was forever, I'd strangle him. All I need to do is go one more day than he does. If I remember that, I can manage."

One morning, SIX MONTHS after his assault had begun, Scott bounced into the kitchen chatting and filled with puns. Kathleen and I watched in amazement. She looked at me saying,

K: "Looks like you made it!"

M: "Made what?"

K: (Turning to look at her brother, tears rolling down her cheeks) "One more day."

There have been few "free rides" with the children's adjustment to the change of divorce, and I see both Kathleen and Scott are stronger for having had this unfortunate experience.

LET YOUR CHILDREN DEVELOP THEIR OWN RELATIONSHIP WITH THEIR (FATHER/MOTHER)

> Essential Ingredients:
> Lack of Ego • Patience • Compassion

Remember: Your children need to learn to stand up in a divorce as much as you do.

Your children do not understand divorce. They will try everything they can to involve you in their new relationship with their (father/mother). They may even resort to causing fights between the two of you — believing that fighting will clear the air so you will get back together again.

In our case, the children went to their father's home every other week-end. He would honk out in front and refused to come into the house. When the week-end was over, two angry defiant, weepy children were returned. My conversation with Kathleen and Scott went something like this:

A: "Dad's a (blank!)."

B: "You're really angry with Dad."

A: "Well, he makes you eat everything at dinner but he doesn't let you choose what you put on your plate"

B: "Looks like you need to use your words and talk to Dad about that."

A: "Will you talk to him?"

B: "No, this is your problem with Dad. You need to talk to him.

A: "He'll get mad if I talk to him.

B: "Dad's mad at everyone right now. You need to talk to him anyway. Do you want to pretend I'm Dad and practice how you will talk to him?"

A: "No. I'm not going to talk to him."

B: "Whatever you choose. The situation won't change because Dad doesn't know the problem exists. Let me know if you change your mind."

As the mother, the last thing I need to do is to take sides and agree that Dad is a (blank). The normal result of that action is that the child ends up being defensive for the ex-mate and sides with him/her against you. The child should not be asked to choose between the two adults in terms of love and allegiance.

CREATING AN INDEPENDENT FAMILY BOND

> Essential Ingredients:
> Communication • Respect • Truth

Remember: Your children are your children, not your saviors in a divorce.

When the family unit is disrupted by divorce, one place is left empty — usually the space of the father. It is very difficult not to ask one of your children to fill that space in some way. Doing so robs that child of his/her own place.

The truth needs to be spoken, but not all of the facts in the truth. "Are you upset, Mom?" does not need, "No, I'm fine," if it is a lie. Say instead, "I'm feeling weepy. I just need to cry a little. Thanks for the hug, now I need some space to work this out for myself."

A: "Are you mad at Daddy?"
B: "Yes, I am. But this is your dad's and my problem to work out. I know you don't like it when we fight. We are trying to learn to talk to each other about our problems."

A: "Is Dad mad at you?"
B: "Yes he is. Neither one of us wants to be divorced, but this is what we need to do. It's our problem to work this out. Dad is not mad at you. I am not mad at you."

It is easy for everyone to go their separate ways when a divorce happens. The children end up eating in front of the TV because the mother doesn't want to deal with their sadness or anger, so the family bond withers and dies. My steadfast rule is that we always eat dinner together at the table with nothing but our conversation as entertainment. No one leaves until everyone is finished and no phone calls are taken. It is our time together. Exceptions occur, and yet our dinner meal is most often together.

A minimum of once a week, I spend one-to-one time with each child. No two children go through divorce the same way. Rather than making assumptions, I talk with and listen to my children.

I did not ask Scott to become the man of the house. He is a boy, not a man.

CHORES

> Essential Ingredients:
> Communication • Perseverance • Humor

Remember: Motivating a child through guilt builds a wall between you and your child.

Scott was nine, Kathleen eleven when we got our divorce. I told the children it was impossible for me to do everything and earn money, so we made a list of all the jobs. They decided they could do their own wash. At first, they combined wash and one did the light colors while the other did the dark colors. This plan made one child dependent upon the other, so they fought about it too much . They decided to change the plan and take care of their own wash. Each one does his/her own towels and sheets once a week as well. In the beginning, I would remind them that the wash needed to be done (usually on the week-end). Reminding soon became unnecessary.

Both children's joke is that the things they give me to be ironed will be outgrown before I do it! So, I bought Kathleen an ironing board that sits on the floor and an iron that shuts itself off. Kathleen taught Scott how to iron, and I ceased to have either the ironing or washing job.

Sometimes, especially when I've been out of town, the house needs more than hit and run assistance. At dinner I say, "I need (two hours) of assistance from both of you this weekend, and want us to make an agreement as to when that will be. The house needs some attention, and it won't take all day." We make an agreement and we all work together to create a pleasant home environment.

If a job needs to be done on a certain day (trash taken out on Wednesday morning) and the person responsible for that job can't do it, the children trade jobs — or just cover for each other. Communication is the key to success in the area of chores and commitment.

> A Friendly Reminder from Mom:
>
> *To be completed prior to dinner time on Sunday:*
>
> ✔ 1. Your room (good luck!)
> ✔ 2. Your bathroom
> ✔ 3. Vacuum the whole house

THE REWARDS AND MEMORIES

KEEP LOTS OF KEEPSAKES

Essential Ingredients:
Plan Ahead • Follow-through • Humor

Remember: By remembering their past children get a chance to appreciate the wonder of their growth.

Each of my two children has a scrapbook filled with photos and comments from me. These books begin at birth and somehow dwindle off in the early teen years. Kathleen has started her own vast collection of memories.

My own collection of photos are in collages hung in the hall to my bedroom. Rather than buying the pre-made type with only a few spaces for photos, I make a giant collage of overlapping photos. Now and then we each stop to look at them.

In my filing cabinet, one whole drawer is divided into a section for Scott and one for Kathleen. Everything from grade cards to notes is in those sections. There is an occasional story one of them wrote, lots of drawings, a unique photo, a special note to their father or me, and even something as silly as a favorite cartoon from that time. I love to hear the two of them laughing as they weed through the items — remembering.

In my daily journal, I have recorded the children's precious moments and conversations. The "Sandy Thoughts" section in my computer (journals are transferred to my computer) is a favorite place for both children to go to read and laugh — and remember.

Kathleen and I have written each other poems and letters over the years. A special folder holds evidence of our love and dedication to building bridges between each other.

Unfortunately, we did not have video cameras available to us, so the past is recorded for us in cassette tapes and lots of photographs. There is a certain amount of magic that is lost in stills — the investment in a video camera is worthwhile.

Every once in awhile, my great big gown-up teenagers will pile all over me, requesting, "Tell us a story about when we were little, Mom."

When Kathleen was little, I would tuck her in, rubbing her arm, while singing "Christopher Robin is Saying His Prayers." Recently, after a day anyone would deem as being difficult, she wearily went to bed. I sat beside her, rubbing her arm as she moaned a little. "Mom, sing Christopher Robin, please," she asked, and through gently falling tears, I did so. Give your children lots of loving memories.

CAPTURE THE WONDER OF THEIR SMALLNESS FOREVER

> Essential Ingredients:
> Tape or Video Recorder • Patience • Listening

Remember: You think you will always remember those little voices and cute sayings, but you don't. Recording them is a source of togetherness and joy for the whole family.

My children were small prior to the advent of video recording, so we captured the joys of their youth on cassette tape. I hung a microphone over the area where the two of them ate their breakfast and lunch. Turning on the machine was easy, and they got used to the microphone so didn't pay any attention to it.

At sixteen and nineteen, Scott and Kathleen found some tapes in a shoe box. I was delighted with the sounds of endless laughter as they sat on the floor in her bedroom (there is no floor visible in his bedroom), listening to tapes.

In the beginning, the tapes were primarily of the adults trying to get the young child to talk. Even that is funny!

Childhood is a magical time of wonder where everything is possible and the best is just beginning. Watching your child's growth and development can reassure you that your investment of time and caring has ample rewards. For the children themselves, it is wonderful to see themselves as trusting, open, zestful tiny humans — all too soon, they get "adult-erated" and with it goes their spontaneity.

The investment of a video or cassette recorder will bring returns to all of you that you can't imagine. Don't wait! Tomorrow some of their "smallness" may be gone.

Remember to keep a file for each child and put school papers, grade cards, notes and drawings into it. Both of my children like to get out their file and go through it — remembering — seeing the wonder of their own growth and development.

HONORING YOUR CHILD'S WISDOM

> Essential Ingredients:
> Listening • Overviewing • Appreciating

Remember: When trusted and respected, children may show a wisdom far beyond their years.

Kathleen was fifteen when she wrote an essay for school about how my mothering has influenced and assisted her. I am grateful that the essay was filled with positives and few negatives. In her essay Kathleen wrote this concerning friendships, **"The distance walked together depends upon the value of lessons we teach each other."**

Scott: "How was your day today, Mom?"
Mom: "OK"
Scott: "Better or worse than yesterday?"
Mom: "Worse."
Scott: "What did you do to make it worse?"
Mom: (laughing) "Lots of things."
Scott: "Good thing there's tomorrow, huh?"

One time, weeping miserably about something in my life, Scott walked into my den. He wrapped a giant arm around me. To my, "I've been talking and talking to God, and I just don't know the answer!" he replied, "Mom, have you been listening to God?"

Having watched a basketball game and seen for myself the emotional abuse given to Scott by his Varsity coach, I was enraged. Storming around in the kitchen, I began talking in terms of what I would like to do to the guy. Kathleen sat in the corner of the sink listening. Finally, she spoke, "You know, you taught us to ask for help when we need it. Maybe Scott isn't asking for help because he doesn't need it now."

Told it was safe, Kathleen swam out in the middle of nine giant bat rays in a bay in Tahiti. Her eyes filled with light as she searched for the words to hold her experience, "Mom, you can't imagine how I felt, diving down as those huge harmless creatures surrounded me! I kept watching them, being careful not to move suddenly and scare them. They were so graceful and trusting. And, Mom, they were five times bigger than I am! I can't tell you how I felt." Her eyes told me.

Recently, I was talking to Scott and watched him casually drop a pearl of wisdom into my life. Leaving the room, I patted his arm saying, "Sometimes I wonder if you or I are the teacher in this home." As I reached the door, a gentle voice followed me, "Someone taught me how to teach."

RECORD THE PRECIOUS MOMENTS

> Essential Ingredients:
> Perseverance • Patience • Sense of Humor

Remember: There are lots and lots of difficult times in raising a child. Capturing their magical moments is a treasure for both you and your child.

From my 1982 journal:

I was sitting there in my finest outfit, hoping he would notice. His eyes twinkled as he stood before me, "You look lovely tonight, may I have this dance?"

I rose, took the arm he offered and walked proudly to the dance floor.

"Can you waltz?" he asked.

"Only with a prince," I responded

"Here I am!" he beamed, and slipped his hand around my waist.

We waltzed, the prince and I, oblivious to on-lookers or other dancers. At one point I said, "keep doing what you are doing, I'll throw in a little twirl." I went out, around and right back into step.

The prince smiled, leaned in closer and asked, "Could you do that again?"

"Certainly," I replied and did.

Returning me to my chair, he bowed slightly and spoke. "Thank you for the dance." As he turned to walk away he added, "...and for being my mom."

I watched my ten year old son cross the room. He was tall, straight and definitely charming. Could that have been the kid with the always-grubby-knees, the room so catastrophically disorderly you needed a guide (or psychologist) to enter — the same kid who yesterday rendered the whole neighborhood defenseless in the Guinness-pleasing spit wad fight; using several rolls of toilet paper and a couple of gallons of water?

This prince with whom I've waltzed — could he be the other kid as well? I don't know....and they certainly look alike....in some ways.

MEMORIES ARE FOREVER

> Essential Ingredients:
> Compassion • Kindness • Understanding

• **Hands Across America:** We traveled in two cars to join with literally hundreds of people, gathering in an otherwise barren part of the world, to celebrate hope and caring. Scott climbed the steep hill and sat alone for an hour. His explanation: "Mom, you can cry and show your feelings. I just wanted to be alone." Later, he had the whole line doing the can-can, making waves, and sent a hug (passed along) that probably reached the cities. This day, I saw a particle of the goodness of my son.

• **Kathleen was in first grade.** I went to her school to see an awards ceremony. Before the program began, she popped up on her knees, systematically searching the gathered parents. When she saw me, she pointed to her eye, to her heart and then put two fingers up like horns on her head. After school, I said, "I got the 'I love you' part of your message, but what does that last one mean?" Giving me her special tolerating-an-adult-look, she added, "Dearly!" To this day, we exchange our message of love in those hand gestures. I point to myself and show two fingers in response. (Me, too!)

• **Conversation with Scott, second grade:**

> Mom: "Scott you need to take a make-up photo at school."
> Scott: "No way! Not me!"
> Mom: "Say more about those feelings, please."
> Scott: "No one is going to put make up on me and take my picture!"

(He had missed picture day so needed to have his school photo taken.)

• **Excerpt from 1988 letter from Kathleen to her mother:** "Sometimes, I think it is hard for me to open up and share my emotions with you. I think there is a reason for this. I see so much of you inside of me that I think it is hard for me to talk to you at times. A lot of times, I haven't wanted to face certain emotions, and when talking to you I feel as if I am also confronting myself. I never wanted to shut you out, and I appreciate the space you give to me."

• **1978:** Kathleen (8) and Julie were playing happily in Kathleen's room. Scott burst through the door, dove on the bed, rolled off onto the floor, crashing into the bookcase. A blank look on his face, he shrugged his shoulders saying, "I forgot what I was going to say," and left.

The girls never discontinued their activity. When Scott left, Kathleen said, "See what I have to live with!" Julie sympathetically muttered, "Yeah."

LETTERS FROM ME TO KATHLEEN AND SCOTT:

Remember: You cannot support your children too much in their attempt to become productive individuals in a complex world.

December 1988

Letting go has to do with beliefs, by the way, not physical happenings. By letting go of Clipper (dog) you give up the idea that love, which was ardent, without judgment and always loyal, can cause pain. The pain is letting go of the illusion of words like "lost" or "irreplaceable" or "gone".

Life is a series of sunsets — you can take a picture of each one, but you cannot capture or repeat them. Each one is a gift to open your heart to greater possibilities of this word "life." If you try to hold onto a sunset, it passes anyway; any pain you feel is self-inflicted. Otherwise, you would wait openly and enthusiastically for the next "sunset," and have no sadness that the one before you has ended. Besides, is a sunset the end of a day or the beginning of night, or is it simply a sunset? Perspective. All of life is perspective and attitude.

I love you dearly,

MOM

Christmas 1988

...What I really wanted you to do was to tell me I'm not a failure because I'm at this impasse in my life, that I won't let you two down, that we will have enough money to live comfortably, and that being a good mother is enough. Every one of those decisions is mine and only mine to make. You answered the one about my mothering by staying in you and telling the truth when I slimed you with my melodrama. It is my own standards which keep me as the judge and jury to my success and failure as a parent, provider and human being.

...I apologize for all the words, but not for all the thoughts. All I can really give you is my thoughts about life so you can structure your own belief system. Looking at what you have accomplished in the few years you've been here, I am amazed, astounded and appreciative of all you have chosen to be.

...And my Darlings, no matter what I or anyone else shares with you in terms of perspective, always to your own dreams be true.

I love you dearly!

MOM

"YOU'RE GOD'S BEST INVENTION."

FOR MOM
ON HER BIRTHDAY
1986

When I was little
You held my hand
And told me about
The things I saw.

A balloon was a spaceship
Carrying angels up to God,
A rose was a paintbrush
On the mural of nature;

The moon was a nightlight
So Santa would know when it was
        safe to come down the chimney
                for all were asleep;

My teddy bear was my guardian angel
Who came alive the moment I left the room,
A mean old man was only scared to love
And had a heart of pure gold;

A sandcastle was a special home
For all my mermaid friends,
The dragon was conquerable
Only shower him with love,
And a clown
Was your hope for the world;

You gave me my imagination
By helping me always to see with love,
And I thank you
For letting go of my hand.

        I love you dearly!

        Kathleen

Scott's Pledge of Allegiance—typed as written
Mrs. Slaughter—2nd Grade
October 23, 1980

```
The Pleige


    I plige ove olegese to the flag ove
united stas ove amicaca and to the
republec for wich stans one nashen under
god induvesubul with liderte and gustes
for all
```

SCOTT'S 1989 CHRISTMAS LETTER TO KATHLEEN

Although
  this card does
    not really fit
      the occasion, I felt
        that you would like it
          just the same. All this room
            gives me a chance to tell you
I love you like you were my <u>real sister</u> *(JK)
  but I must say I am really glad that
    you were left on our doorstep and not someone
      else's. You turned out to be a truly terrific
        sister. Ya know all my friends that have
          sisters or brothers, they usually never
            even talk to each other let alone share
              like we do. Well, to make a longer
                story just long, I am grateful
                  you are my sister, and
                    I love you very much.
                      Your little bro, Scott

* (JK)=Just Kidding

A Poem about Scott
1976

THE STEM

Please be kind enough not to ask
Why that stem sits alone in its vase,
It's not the refuse of flowers
Or something to occupy space.

Some folks laugh when they look at it,
When I see it even I must smile;
It's a gift you see from my son
Which arrived via crocodile.

It was once a total flower,
A pansy, a mum or a daisy;
When I asked him where he picked it
I found his memory hazy.

He remembers jungles and swamps,
Crossing valleys and mountains steep,
Forded a river on a raft,
Although frightened he did not weep.

He stood before me exhausted,
His clothes in complete disarray,
"Mom I picked this flower for you,
But lost some of it on the way."

Please be kind enough not to ask
Why that stem sits alone in its vase,
A flower of imagination
Deserves a very special place.

Love,
Mom

SCOTTIE

A curb is a bridge over a gorge,
Trees are an escape from lions,
Puddles are filled with crocodiles,
And crack-steppers get eaten by bears;
To hide from monsters get under the slide,
From dragons a table will do;
Being all boy simply means
He has an imagination.

Kathleen

Get them up,
　　Change their clothes,
　　　　Give them milk to drink;
　　　　　　Change their diapers,
　　　　　　　Wipe their faces,
　　　　　　　　Tuck them in for naps;

Play with them, sing to them,
　　Oops! It's time for bath!
　　　　Dinner time, changing pants
　　　　　　Does the routine ever end?

I shake my head when people say
　　Being a kid is all play;
　　　　There's a lot of time and work involved
　　　　　　In being a mother to dolls.

SANDY McDANIEL WORKSHOPS

Internationally-known *SPEAKER   AUTHOR*
PUBLISHER   CONSULTANT
EDUCATOR   ENTREPRENEUR
PRESIDENT SMC ENTERPRISES
PARENT - TWO TEENAGERS

KEYNOTE ADDRESS • EXPERIENTIAL WORKSHOPS • TALKS

- Graduate University of Redlands
- Co-Author, Project Self-Esteem, a K-6 program in 48 states and international.
- Author & Publisher: <u>Recipes From Parenting</u>
- Fourteen years as a national and international presenter
- Recipient: Disneyland Community Service Award, National PTA Honorary Service Award, Chamber of Commerce Silver Anchor Award, National Council for Self-Esteem's Golden Apple Award.

<u>**Partial List of Topics:**</u> (Meeting individual needs is her comitment)

Are You Tired of Being the Warden?
(Parenting: Children of all ages)

Enhancing Self-Esteem
Enhancing Learning Through Self-Esteem
Leadership Training for Teenagers
Self-Esteem, the Bottom Line for Drug Prevention
Enhancing Children's Potential
(4 - 12) Steps for Personal Success
Building Customer Relations

"Sandy is the most dynamic, warm, inspiring presenter I know. Those who have the opportunity to attend one of her workshops/talks consider themselves fortunate and truly enriched."

Connie Dembrowski,
Chairperson National Council for Self-Esteem

"Sandy is a warm, intelligent individual who is very effective in assisting employees in becoming more self-assured in their personal and professional lives."

Joseph Bernhardt,
Vice President First Interstate Bank

P.O. Box 15458, Newport Beach, CA 92659 • (714) 642-3605

"I Wish I had owned Recipes from Parenting many years ago!"
Og Mandino, Author of <u>The Greatest Salesman in the World</u>,
<u>The Greatest Miracle in the World</u>, etc.

"As a Family Life Counselor for a school district, this book has been a God-send for helping me give parents alternative parenting strategies. It has also been a resource for me as a step-mom; sometimes what we know professionally is difficult to apply in our own lives."
Sandy Atwood, New York

"This book puts things into perspective and inspires me to empathize with my children. Recipes from Parenting reminds me I am not alone in my concerns, and wraps usable solutions in so much warmth and humor that it is a joy to read and re-read each page."
Claire Belden (four children ages 7,5,3 & 2)

"My father-in-law, being from the 'old school' has often been critical of our parenting techniques. After he read your book he said, 'I should have read this book forty years ago!' He now understands so much of what we are trying to do. He says it is the only book without a plot that has kept him spellbound. Now my problem has changed; whenever I do something inappropriate he says, 'Remember what Sandy said!' Please encourage grandparents everywhere to read Recipes from Parenting."
Kathy Klaus, Pennsylvania

"Thank you for writing such a helpful book; It is a superb gift for baby showers, friends, relatives and business associates."
Dona Constantine, Emergency Nurses Association, Orange County, CA

ORDER MORE COPIES TODAY ! ! ! ! ! ! ! ! ! ! !

Send.....

$12.95 + $.80 CA tax per book
plus $ 2.00 handling per book for 1st item;
$ 1.00 for each additional item
to:

SANDY MCDANIEL ENTERPRISES

P.O. Box 15458
Newport Beach, CA 92659